Quotable

NEW
ENGLANDER

Quotable

NEW ENGLANDER

Four Centuries of Wit and Wisdom

ERIC D. LEHMAN

Globe
Pequot

Guilford, Connecticut

Globe
Pequot

An imprint of The Rowman & Littlefield Publishing Group, Inc.
4501 Forbes Blvd., Ste. 200
Lanham, MD 20706
www.rowman.com

Distributed by NATIONAL BOOK NETWORK

Copyright © 2019 Eric D. Lehman

British Library Cataloguing in Publication Information available

Library of Congress Cataloging-in-Publication Data available

ISBN 978-1-4930-3611-0 (paperback)
ISBN 978-1-4930-3612-7 (e-book)

♾™ The paper used in this publication meets the minimum requirements of American National Standard for Information Sciences—Permanence of Paper for Printed Library Materials, ANSI/NISO Z39.48-1992.

Printed in the United States of America

CONTENTS

ACKNOWLEDGMENTS

Thanks to my editor, Amy Lyons, who suggested this project, and to my wife, Amy Nawrocki, for all her support and help. Special thanks to my research assistants and friends for sorting through hundreds of thousands of quotes for the ones that made the cut: Danya Alkhatib, Jessica Taylor, Qetarah Richardson, and David and Trena Lehman. After all, as Amos Bronson Alcott said, "One must be a wise reader to quote wisely and well."

INTRODUCTION

The idea of New England is four centuries old. The arrival of the Puritans, the influence of local Native Americans, and the successive waves of immigration created this unique culture east of the Hudson River and south of the St. Lawrence valley. Forged in the fires of the Great Awakening, the American Revolution, and the Industrial Revolution, the emerging New Englanders became iconic throughout the world, due to both their distinct character and their global impact. Emigrants from our six states went on to settle western New York, Michigan, Ohio, and beyond, creating and influencing a lion's share of American culture.

Surely the thick sinews of these pioneers no longer tether the bones of today's suburbanites. Or do they? Every time a tragedy strikes or a challenge is offered, today's New Englanders seem to step up to the plate, to rise to the occasion, to speak the words that are needed. There must be a certain quality to the soils here, in the river clay or in the beach sand. Perhaps it is the salt of the North Atlantic, blown into our bodies by the spray. Or could it have been absorbed into our bodies through the cranberries, the maple syrup, or the clam chowder?

Whatever the case, no one can deny that this land has birthed a certain quality of voice different from anywhere else in the world. We can hear it today in the chatter of bustling taverns or college classrooms, in the slow drawl of the farmer and the nasal pause of the Eastern establishment. It contains the dropped "Rs" of our north, the dropped "Ts" of our south. The words we use were tested by our knitting circles and printed in our rural newspapers before being polished by the *Harvard Lampoon* or the *New England Journal of Medicine*. The roots of this language may have originated in Old England long ago, but they also echo the cry of seagulls, the laugh of loons, the trilling notes of the white-throated sparrow. It includes the music of fifes, the roll of drums, and the cracks of bats in Fenway Park. Waves of immigrants from places like Ireland, Italy, and Latin America added their own voices to the symphony. Or was it the other way around? Perhaps this land and its culture make you part of them; the immigrants in Providence find themselves saying very different things from their former compatriots in Parsippany or Pittsburgh.

It is also undeniable that we have a lot to say—about our landscapes and weather, about our peoples and cultures, about life and love. But this has mingled with a natural quietness, a Yankee thriftiness with words. What results is a careful crafting of language seldom equaled. As Robert Frost put it in a commencement address at Oberlin College in 1937: "The thing New England gave most to America was the thing I am talking about: a stubborn clinging to meaning—to purify words until they meant again what they should mean." What results from this "clinging to meaning" are thousands of perfect quotations.

Searching the internet will not usually yield genuine quotations. A quotation is not an image or a rhyme or an anecdote; it is a complete thought told simply. It could be an affirmation or a negation, an argument or an announcement, an attitude or an aphorism. But a quotation is not a song, no matter how memorable, though a rhyme may form the statement. It is not descriptive and not a feeling, though it may contain both descriptive details and feelings. It is not a personal story, though a story may contain a significant quotation.

There are other combinations of words by New Englanders deserving of note—in the lines of poetry, the paragraphs of novels, the research papers of scientists. There are great jokes and insults and stories. And of course, there are gray areas—a statement may be made in a way that is not declarative. A quotation may be in-between the lines, in the pauses and the questions. Nevertheless, a quotation is first and foremost an expression of a thought, in language as clear as a Maine mountain lake.

What follows in this book are the clearest expressions in writing or speech made by New Englanders, both present and former, who remain some of the most quotable people in the world. Here you might find an old proverb that you thought your grandmother invented, or a new saying that will become your mantra. There is wisdom here, and humor, and phrases that might bring a tear to your eye. These are the words you've always been waiting to hear.

CHAPTER 1

Wisdom
and Wit

Quotes by New Englanders that have enriched the American soul

In the early 1800s the "Yankee" from New England became the first American "type" to find popularity as a "wit" in other areas of the country and as far away as Europe—a homespun farmer whittling a block of wood and chatting amiably about the topics of the day. By the end of the century, represented by such titanic figures as P. T. Barnum and Mark Twain, these Yankee wits became the image of our entire nation at home and abroad (before "cowboys" took them over). Twenty-first century wit Seth Meyers called this characteristic a "sort of wry New England sense of pointing out anyone who's trying to make a big deal of himself."

We are thinkers, large and small. We tend toward philosophy, because we philosophize more than any other area of the country. The clever turns of phrase and homespun wisdom of our shrewd, hearty folk have been collected in Ralph Waldo Emerson's *Essays* and Benjamin Franklin's *Poor Richard's Almanack*. And they live on in every farm kitchen and stainless-steel diner, where we sip our coffee and read our newspapers. We discuss the matters of the day, we consider, we pronounce. If that is wisdom, then we have more than our share. If it is merely wit, why, then, as sometime Cape Codder Kurt Vonnegut said, "So it goes."

* * *

Practical politics consists in ignoring facts.

—Henry Adams,
The Education of Henry Adams

Facts are stubborn things; and whatever may be our wishes, our inclinations, or the dictates of our passions, they cannot alter the state of facts and evidence.

—John Adams, argument in defense of the soldiers
in the Boston Massacre, December 1770

Show me a good loser, and I'll show you a loser.

—Arnold "Red" Auerbach, coach of the Boston Celtics

Fight fire with fire.

—P. T. Barnum, showman, *Struggles and Triumphs*

Part-time information and full-time opinions can be very dangerous.

—Chris Berman, announcer for ESPN

To achieve great things, two things are needed: a plan and not quite enough time.

—Leonard Bernstein, composer and conductor

That which easily comes as freely goes.

—Anne Bradstreet, *Tenth Muse*

The truth is always exciting. Speak it, then. Life is dull without it.

—Pearl S. Buck, author

There's no substitute for hard work and effort beyond the call of duty.
—Walter Camp, father of American football

Fix your eyes on perfection and you make almost everything speed towards it.

—William Ellery Channing, preacher and theologian

A party without cake is just a meeting.
　　　　　　　　　—Julia Child, chef and television host

If you don't say anything, you won't be called on to repeat it.
　　　—Calvin Coolidge, 30th president of the United States

I think a human animal is far more wild and unpredictable
and dangerous and destructive than any other animal.
　　　　　—Jeff Corwin, biologist and wildlife conservationist

Humanity I love you because when you're hard up you pawn
your intelligence to buy a drink.
　　　　　　　　　　—e. e. cummings, "La Guerre"

Attempt the impossible in order to improve your work.
　　　　　　　　　　　—Bette Davis, actress

Hope is the thing with feathers
That perches in the soul
And sings the tune without the words—
And never stops at all.
　　　　　　　　—Emily Dickinson, "Poem no. 254"

The return from your work must be the satisfaction which
that work brings you and the world's need of that work.
　　　—W. E. B. Du Bois, "To His Newborn Great-Grandson"

Philosophy accepts the hard and hazardous task of dealing with problems not yet open to the methods of science—problems like good and evil, beauty and ugliness, order and freedom, life and death.

—Will Durant, historian, *The Story of Philosophy*

I believe in rules. Sure I do. If there weren't any rules, how could you break them?

—Leo Durocher, former Major League Baseball player, *Nice Guys Finish Last*

Sin makes its own hell, and goodness its own heaven.

—Mary Baker Eddy, religious leader, *Science and Health*

I assert that nothing ever comes to pass without a cause.

—Jonathan Edwards, preacher and theologian, *Freedom of the Will*

Where you think you are going is your destination, but your destiny is where you actually find yourself.

—John Elder, *Reading the Mountains of Home*

Beauty, what is that? . . . Beauty neither buys food nor keeps up a home.

—Maxine Elliott, actress

Trust thyself. Each heart vibrates to an iron string.
—Ralph Waldo Emerson, *Self-Reliance*

Doubt is the brother of shame.
—Erik Erikson, psychologist,
"The Problem of Ego Identity"

It's not what you achieve, it's what you overcome.
—Carlton Fisk, former catcher for the Boston Red Sox

Early to bed and early to rise, makes a man healthy, wealthy,
and wise.
—Benjamin Franklin, inventor,
Poor Richard's Almanack

Every builder builds somewhat for unknown purposes, and
is in a measure a prophet.
—Mary E. Wilkins Freeman, "The Revolt of 'Mother'"

Two roads diverged in a wood, and I—
I took the one less traveled by,
And that has made all the difference.
—Robert Frost, "The Road Not Taken"

Dare to be naïve.
—Buckminster Fuller, inventor, *Moral of the Work*

Genius will live and thrive without training, but it does not the less reward the watering pot and pruning knife.
—Margaret Fuller, *Diary*

You have brains in your head.
You have feet in your shoes.
You can steer yourself
any direction you choose.
—Theodor Seuss Geisel, *Oh, the Places You'll Go!*

The world, unfortunately, rarely matches our hopes and consistently refuses to behave in a reasonable manner.
—Stephen Jay Gould, biologist, *The Panda's Thumb*

The only sure weapon against bad ideas is better ideas.
—A. Whitney Griswold, 16th president of Yale University

Life is made up of marble and mud.
—Nathaniel Hawthorne, *House of Seven Gables*

Cynicism is an unpleasant way of saying the truth.
—Lillian Hellman, *The Little Foxes*

Knowledge and timber shouldn't be used until they are seasoned.
—Oliver Wendell Holmes Sr.,
The Autocrat of the Breakfast Table

Never confuse faith, or belief—of any kind—with
something even remotely intellectual.

—John Irving, *A Prayer for Owen Meany*

The art of being wise is the art of knowing what to overlook.

—William James, philosopher and psychologist,
The Principles of Psychology

Tact is after all a kind of mind-reading.

—Sarah Orne Jewett,
The Country of the Pointed Firs

Write your own part.

—Mindy Kaling, actress

Let us never negotiate out of fear. But let us never fear to
negotiate.

—John F. Kennedy, 35th president of the United States,
Inaugural Address, January 20, 1961

Only those who dare to fail greatly, can ever achieve greatly.

—Robert F. Kennedy, 64th US attorney general,
Day of Affirmation Address, June 6, 1966

Pretty girls make graves.

—Jack Kerouac, *The Dharma Bums*

Kick it up a notch!

 —Emeril Lagasse, chef and television host

Turn on, tune in, drop out.

 —Timothy Leary, psychologist

Failure seldom stops you. What stops you is the fear of failure.

 —Jack Lemmon, actor

If you go through life and no one hates you, that means you're not good at anything.

 —Paul Michael Levesque (Triple H), wrestler

One cannot collect all the beautiful shells on the beach.

 —Anne Morrow Lindbergh, *Gift from the Sea*

Do not cross the bridge until you come to it.

 —Henry Wadsworth Longfellow, *Journal*

The most merciful thing in the world, I think, is the inability of the human mind to correlate all its contents.

 —H. P. Lovecraft, "The Call of Cthulhu"

All the beautiful sentiments in the world weigh less than a single lovely action.

 —James Russell Lowell, poet

Happiness equals reality minus expectations.
—Tom Magliozzi, radio host, *Car Talk*

Be ashamed to die until you have won some victory for humanity.
—Horace Mann, educator, Commencement Address at Antioch College, 1859

Upon the first advice of any Abuse offered unto you, resolve. I will keep my Mouth with a Bridle, while I have before me what the unbridled Mouth of Wickedness has uttered of me.
—Cotton Mather, minister

I know that you believe you understand what you think I said, but I'm not sure you realize that what you heard is not what I meant.
—Robert McCloskey, author

Climb the mountain so you can see the world, not so the world can see you.
—David McCullough, historian

A smile is the chosen vehicle of all ambiguities.
—Herman Melville, *Pierre*

A man always has two reasons for what he does—a good
one, and the real one.
—John Pierpont Morgan Sr., financier and banker

Mediocrity is like a spot on your shirt, it never comes off.
—Haruki Murakami, *Dance Dance Dance*

When all else fails, there's always delusion.
—Conan O'Brien, television host

There is always one dream left, one final dream,
no matter how low you have fallen, down there
at the bottom of the bottle.
—Eugene O'Neill, playwright

If they want you to cook the dinner, at least they ought to let
you shop for some of the groceries.
—Bill Parcells, former coach of the New England
Patriots, on not being given money

Some things can be done as well as others.
—Sam Patch, first American daredevil

Great cooking favors the prepared hands.
—Jacques Pepin, chef and television host

11

Don't give up the ship.
—Oliver Hazard Perry, US naval officer, War of 1812

Frequently the more trifling the subject, the more animated and protracted the discussion.
—Franklin Pierce, 14th president of the United States

They who dream by day are cognizant of many things which escape those who dream only by night.
—Edgar Allan Poe, "Eleonora"

No matter where you go, there you are.
—Earl Mac Rauch, screenwriter, *The Adventures of Buckaroo Banzai Across the 8th Dimension*

A minute lived attentively can contain a millennium; an adequate step can span the planet.
—Chet Raymo, *The Path*

You can think of a lot of things to make out of nothing, if you have to.
—Louise Dickinson Rich, *We Took to the Woods*

Work is a sovereign remedy for all ills, and a man who loves to work will never be unhappy.
—Ellen Swallow Richards, industrial engineer at Massachusetts Institute of Technology

A nation without humor is not only sad but dangerous.
—Abby Aldrich Rockefeller, philanthropist

Sometimes we choose our challenges, and at other times our challenges choose us.
—Travis Roy, former hockey player for Boston University

Those who cannot remember the past are condemned to repeat it.
—George Santayana, *The Life of Reason*

They say any landing you can walk away from is a good one.
—Alan Shepard, astronaut and the first American in space

Your inability to see yourself clearly is what's keeping you alive.
—Sarah Silverman, comedian, *The Bedwetter*

The real problem is not whether machines think but whether men do.
—B. F. Skinner, behavioral psychologist, *Contingencies of Reinforcement*

One of the basic causes for all the trouble in the world today is that people talk too much and think too little.
—Margaret Chase Smith, former US Senator from Maine

You know more than you think you do.
—Benjamin Spock, pediatrician,
Dr. Spock's Baby and Child Care

Ultimately, we're all responsible for putting our belief into action.

—Paul Stookey, singer

All the wondrous physical, intellectual and moral endowments, with which man is blessed, will, by inevitable law, become useless, unless he uses and improves them. . . . If a love for truth and beauty and goodness is not cultivated, the mind loses the strength which comes from truth, the refinement which comes from beauty, and the happiness which comes from goodness.

—Anne Sullivan, teacher, Commencement Address at Perkins School for the Blind, 1886

Every adult is a teacher.

—Harold Tantaquidgeon, Mohegan Chief

The journey, not the arrival matters;
the voyage not the landing.
—Paul Theroux, *The Old Patagonian Express*

Aim above morality. Be not simply good; be good for something.

—Henry David Thoreau, *Walden*

You can't pray a lie.
　　　　—Mark Twain, *The Adventures of Huckleberry Finn*

Some days you're the bug, some days you're the windshield.
　　　　　　　　　　　—Steven Tyler, singer

That's one of the tragedies of this life—that the men who
are most in need of a beating up are always enormous.
　　　　　　　　　　—Rudy Vallee, singer and actor

Deep breaths are very helpful at shallow parties.
　　　　—Barbara Walters, broadcast journalist, *How to Talk
　　　　with Practically Anybody about Practically Anything*

Inconsistencies of opinion, arising from changes of
circumstances, are often justifiable.
　　—Daniel Webster, former US senator from Massachusetts,
　　　　　　　　　　　"Speech, July 25, 1846"

It was easy enough to despise the world, but decidedly
difficult to find any other habitable region.
　　　　　　　　　　　—Edith Wharton, author

O Virtue, smiling in immortal green,
Do thou exert thy pow'r, and change the scene;
Be thine employ to guide my future days,
And mine to pay the tribute of my praise.
　　　　　—Phillis Wheatley, "On Recollection"

I'm not arguing with you—I am telling you.
> —James McNeill Whistler, artist,
> *The Gentle Art of Making Enemies*

Safety is all well and good; I prefer freedom.
> —E. B. White, *The Trumpet of the Swan*

Remember that you will never reach a higher standard than you yourself set. Then set your mark high, and step by step even though it be by painful effort by self-denial and sacrifice, ascend the whole length of the ladder of progress.
> —Ellen G. White, co-founder of the
> Seventh-Day Adventist Church

For of all sad words of tongue or pen,
The saddest are these: "It might have been!"
> —John Greenleaf Whittier, "Maud Muller"

Men's consciences ought in no sort be violated, urged or constrained.
> —Roger Williams, theologian, founder of
> Rhode Island, "Address to Parliament"

If you don't think too good, don't think too much.
—Ted Williams, former outfielder for the Boston Red Sox

If you strive for the moon, maybe you'll get over the fence.
—James Woods, actor

A clear conscience is usually the sign of a bad memory.
—Steven Wright, comedian

I hope the time will never come when I shall feel satisfied.
To reach the goal of one's ambitions must be tragic.
—N. C. Wyeth, artist

CHAPTER 2

Swamp Yankees and Ivy Leaguers

Quotes about the peoples of New
England and their character

From the Mayflower's landing to the age of the internet,
the people of New England have always had something to
say. But who are those people? Do we mean the fisher-folk
and forest-clearers of the early decades, the rich Boston
brahmins of the 19th century, or the industrial workers
of the early 20th? Do we mean the most profoundly educated people in the country? Or just the people living in
the nicest suburbs? Ellen Swallow Richards of MIT put

it this way: "New England is the home of all that is good and noble with all her sternness and uncompromising opinions." This backhanded compliment shows clearly how we have seen ourselves for the last few centuries. We know what we know, and we know it best.

However, that aphorism also exposes a contradiction. We pioneered one of the bedrocks of democracy, the town meeting, yet we also helped pioneer the rights of privacy. Few have expressed this tension in our nature better than the farmers in Robert Frost's "Mending Wall," who come together, socially, to pile stones between their properties. We are alone, together, one people made up of millions of individuals. No one knows who coined the phrase "There is no 'I' in team," but with a slight blush we must admit that it was probably not a New Englander.

*　*　*

It is not in the still calm of life, or in the repose of a pacific station, that great characters are formed . . . Great necessities call out great virtues.
—Abigail Adams, patriot, "Letter to John Quincy Adams"

Resistance to something was the
law of New England nature.
—Henry Adams,
The Education of Henry Adams

Beware of idleness, luxury, and all vanity, folly and vice.
—John Adams, 2nd president of the United States

Women have been called queens for a long time, but the kingdom given them isn't worth ruling.
—Louisa May Alcott, *An Old-Fashioned Girl*

Rather than fail I will retire with my hardy Green Mountain Boys to the desolate caverns of the mountains, and wage war with human nature at large.
—Ethan Allen, farmer and patriot

The New England conscience does not stop you from doing what you shouldn't—it just stops you from enjoying it.
—Cleveland Amory, author and animal rights activist

If two New Hampshiremen aren't a match for the Devil, we might as well give the country back to the Indians.
—Stephen Vincent Benet, "The Devil and Daniel Webster"

The Yankee mind was quick and sharp, but mainly it was singularly honest.
—Van Wyck Brooks, historian, *The Flowering of New England*

The shades of New England are here on my skin. Brine in the blood, grit in the bones, and sea air in the lungs.
—L. M. Browning, *Fleeting Moments of Fierce Clarity*

Every man is a volume if you know how to read him.
—William Ellery Channing, preacher and theologian

I will work in my own way, according to the light that is in me.
—Lydia Maria Child, activist, "Letter to Ellis Gray Loring"

The courage of New England was the courage of conscience.
—Rufus Choate, lawyer, "Address 1834"

If a man buys what he don't need, I call him extravagant, whether it is an extra acre of land, a two-story bonnet, or a bogus gold watch chain, without any watch. If a man can do business with a wheelbarrow, he should not invest in a horse and cart.
—William Clift, *The Tim Bunker Papers, or Yankee Farming*

I love Vermont because of her hills and valleys, her scenery and invigorating climate, but most of all because of her indomitable people. They are a race of pioneers who almost beggared themselves for others.
—Calvin Coolidge, 30th president of the United States, "Speech at Bennington, 1928"

My parents are both from Vermont, very old-fashioned New England. We heated our house with wood my father chopped. My mom grew all of our food. We were very underexposed to everything.

—Geena Davis, actress

I have a Brother and Sister—My Mother does not care for thought—and a Father, too busy with his Beliefs—to notice what we do—He buys me many Books—but begs me not to read them—because he feels they joggle the Mind.

—Emily Dickinson, "Letter to Thomas Wentworth Higginson, April 15, 1862"

Our Puritan forefathers, though bitterly denouncing all forms and ceremonies, were great respecters of persons; and in nothing was the regard for wealth and position more fully shown than in designating the seat in which each person should sit during public worship.

—Alice Morse Earle, historian

Whoso would be a man must be a nonconformist.

—Ralph Waldo Emerson, *Self-Reliance*

God helps those who help themselves.

—Benjamin Franklin, inventor, *Poor Richard's Almanack*

Nobility of character manifests itself at loop-holes when it is not provided with large doors.

—Mary E. Wilkins Freeman, "The Revolt of 'Mother'"

Yankees are what they always were.
—Robert Frost, "Brown's Descent"

We fight, get beat, rise, and fight again.
—Nathanael Greene, Revolutionary
War general, "Letter, April, 1781"

And the heavy night hung dark,
The hills and waters o'er,
When a band of exiles moored their bark
On the wild New England shore.
—Felicia Hemans, *The Landing of the Pilgrim Fathers*

Country people do not behave as if they think life is short;
they live on the principle that it is long, and savor variations
of the kind best appreciated if most days are the same.
—Edward Hoagland, author

That which is hard to do is best done bitterly.
—John Hodgman, comedian,
More Information Than You Require

Humility is the first of virtues—for other people.
—Oliver Wendell Holmes Sr.,
The Professor at the Breakfast Table

Good habits are worth being fanatical about.
—John Irving, author

Ask not what your country can do for you—ask what you can do for your country.

—John F. Kennedy, 35th president of the
United States, Inaugural Address

Whenever you're sitting across from
some important person, always picture him
sitting there in a suit of long red underwear.
That's the way I always operated in business.
—Joseph P. Kennedy, diplomat

New England: All of the Bitterness, Most of the Boating,
None of the Bulls@#t.

—Caroline Kepnes, *You*

You have to start knowing yourself so well that you begin to
know other people. A piece of us is in every person we can
ever meet.

—Stephen King, *Night Shift*

They are Govern'd by the same Laws as wee in Boston, (or
little differing,) thr'out this whole Colony of Connecticot, And
much the same way of Church Government, and many of them
good, Sociable people, and I hope Religious too: but a little too
much Independant in their principalls, and, as I have been told,
were formerly in their Zeal very Riggid in their Administrations
towards such as their Lawes made Offenders, even to a
harmless Kiss or Innocent merriment among Young people.
—Sarah Kemble Knight, tavern owner, *Journal*

I find each new person whom I meet a complete restatement of what life and the world are all about.

—Edwin Herbert Land, founder of Polaroid

What New England is, is a state of mind, a place where dry humor and perpetual disappointment blend to produce an ironic pessimism that folks from away find most perplexing.

—Willem Lange, author

Maple sugaring exemplifies the classic New England values of connectedness to land and community, Yankee ingenuity, observation of the natural world, heritage pride, entrepreneurship, homespun hospitality, make-do and can-do, and simplicity.

—David K. Leff, *Maple Sugaring: Keeping It Real in New England*

When one is a stranger to oneself then one is estranged from others too.

—Anne Morrow Lindbergh, *Gift from the Sea*

All the things come round to him who will but wait.

—Henry Wadsworth Longfellow, "The Student's Tale; The Falcon of Ser Federigo"

I first drew in New England's air, and from her hardy breast Sucked in the tyrant-hating milk that will not let me rest.

—James Russell Lowell, "On the Capture of Certain Fugitive Slaves Near Washington"

Our humility is what makes us great.

—Tom Magliozzi, radio host, *Car Talk*

Be always really, heartily, inwardly loathing your
self; really esteem others Wiser and Better than
your self; really shun Honours. Be averse to
them, afraid of them; never be uneasy at
being over-looked by other Men.

—Cotton Mather, minister

My kids remind me every day how much I don't know.

—Jo Dee Messina, singer

In Maine we have a saying that there's no point in speaking
unless you can improve on silence.

—Edmund Muskie, 58th secretary of state

It is a common thing, in his country, to meet with a man,
uniting in himself half a dozen trades and professions; having
a tolerable acquaintance with many things, that have no
relationship with one another, and a pretty good knowledge
of some one trade or profession; but very uncommon, to
meet with a man, who is a complete master of any one trade or
profession. The sum of a New Englander's knowledge may be
as great as that of another's, but in almost every case it will be
found less available, and less wisely apportioned.

—John Neal, *Brother Jonathan*

A man with no enemies is a man with no character.
—Paul Newman, actor and philanthropist

If a person is to get to the meaning of life, he must learn
to like the facts about himself—ugly as they may seem to
his sentimental vanity—before he can lay hold on the truth
behind the facts; and that truth is never ugly!
—Eugene O'Neill, playwright

I live in rural New Hampshire, and we are, frankly, short on
people who are black, gay, Jewish, and Hispanic. In fact,
we're short on people. My town has a population of 301.
—P. J. O'Rourke, journalist

What the Puritans gave the world was not thought,
but action.
—Wendell Phillips, lawyer, "The Pilgrims"

Maine people have a live-and-let-live philosophy, and tend
to be fair and open-minded.
—Chellie Pingree, US House
of Representatives from Maine

I'm a good knitter, and I'm proud of it. I see no point in
being modest about things you know you do well. It doesn't
indicate humility so much as hypocrisy or lack of perception.
—Louise Dickinson Rich, *We Took to the Woods*

Some call us American Indians. Others call us Native Americans. But we were here long before this continent was renamed "America." Therefore, we claim the right to determine what it means to be indigenous—to maintain our identity and to be respected for who we are. It's important to understand and respect that there are many ways of being human.

—Trudie Lamb Richmond, leader and
elder, Schaghticoke Tribal Nation

Here in New England, the character is strong and unshakable.

—Norman Rockwell, painter

In Maine, there is a deeply ingrained sense that you can always get a little more use out of something.

—Tim Sample, *Maine Oddities,
Curiosities and Roadside Attractions*

For much of America, the all-American values depicted in Norman Rockwell's classic illustrations are idealistic. For those of us from Vermont, they're realistic. That's what we do.
—Bernie Sanders, US senator from Vermont

Prosperity, alas! is often but another name for pride.

—Lydia Sigourney, "Mistakes"

The pilgrim fathers of New England, and their children
of the first and second generations, are justly renowned
for their grave character, their moral uprightness, which
sometimes was rather more than perpendicular, and the
vigilant circumspection which each one exercised over his
neighbor as well as himself.

—Seba Smith, *Way Down East;
or, Portraitures of Yankee Life*

You can never solve a problem without talking to people
with whom you disagree.

—Olympia Snowe, former US senator from Maine

I grew up on a dirt road in Maine, and pretty much
everybody on that dirt road was related to me, and they were
old. And so grumpy.

—Elizabeth Strout, novelist

Reduce the complexity of life by eliminating the needless
wants of life, and the labors of life reduce themselves.

—Edwin Way Teale, naturalist

Our life is frittered away by detail. . . . Simplify, simplify.

—Henry David Thoreau, *Walden*

Nothing so needs reforming as other peoples' habits.

—Mark Twain, *Pudd'nhead Wilson*

One out of three hundred and twelve Americans
is a bore, for instance, and a healthy male adult
bore consumes each year one and a half times
his own weight in other people's patience.
—John Updike, "Confessions of a Wild Bore"

Let us all be happy, and live within our means, even if we
have to borrer [sic] money to do it with.
—Artemus Ward (Charles Farrar Brown),
Science and Natural History

We are half-ruined by conformity, but we should be wholly
ruined without it.
—Charles Dudley Warner, *My Summer in a Garden*

Identity is not inherent. It is shaped by circumstance and
sensitivity and resistance to self-pity.
—Dorothy West, *The Wedding*

We must delight in each other, make others conditions our
own, rejoice together, mourn together, labor and suffer
together, always having before our eyes our commission
and community in the work, our community as members of
the same body.
—John Winthrop, governor of the Massachusetts
Bay Colony, "A Model of Christian Charity"

From purest wells of English undefiled
None deeper drank than he, the New World's Child,
Who in the language of their farm field spoke
The wit and wisdom of New England folk.

—John Greenleaf Whittier, "James Russell Lowell"

There's a quality of life in Maine which is this singular and
unique. I think. It's absolutely a world onto itself.

—Jamie Wyeth, painter

CHAPTER 3

Liberty and Tyranny

Quotes about the historical and contemporary battles for freedom

New Englanders have always stood at the forefront of the fight for liberty against tyranny. Aren't we the sturdy farmers who stood at Concord, at Lexington, and at Bunker Hill, when Israel Putnam told his men, "Don't fire until you see the whites of their eyes"? Or was that William Prescott? Either way, he was one of ours. And long before the Revolution, these northeastern colonies were founded on the idea of utopia by a small group of people looking for the freedom to create a perfect society, one that could exist separately from the rest of the world, sinless, pure, and at peace.

But even in those early years, battles with Native Americans, oppression of other faiths, and witch hangings were all reminders that one person's utopia could be another's tyranny. And we can often lose the very liberties we fight for by becoming tyrants. As Walt Kelly put it so ominously in the cartoon *Pogo*, "We have met the enemy and they are us." Freedom can be a tricky business, but as long as there are New Englanders on the job, we stand a fighting chance.

* * *

Do not put such unlimited power into the hands of the husbands. Remember, all men would be tyrants if they could.
—Abigail Adams, patriot, "Letter to John Adams, March 31, 1776"

The fundamental article of my political creed is that despotism, or unlimited sovereignty, or absolute power, is the same in a majority of a popular assembly, an aristocratical council, an oligarchical junto, and a single emperor. Equally arbitrary, cruel, bloody, and in every respect diabolical.
—John Adams, 2nd president of the United States, "Letter to Thomas Jefferson, November 13, 1815"

Driven from every other corner of the earth, freedom of thought and the right of private judgment in matters of conscience direct their course to this happy country as their last asylum.

—Samuel Adams, 4th governor of Massachusetts, "Speech in Philadelphia, August 1, 1776"

The Stamp Act was to go into operation on the first day of November. On the previous morning, the "New Hampshire Gazette" appeared with a deep black border and all the typographical emblems of affliction, for was not Liberty dead?

—Thomas Bailey Aldrich, "An Old Town by the Sea"

A monarchy is a merchantman which sails well, but will sometimes strike on a rock, and go to the bottom; a republic is a raft which will never sink, but then your feet are always in the water.

—Fisher Ames, former member of the US House of Representatives from Massachusetts

I have no misgivings about, or lack of confidences in the cause in which I am engaged, and my courage does not falter. I know how strongly American civilization now leans on the triumph of the government, and how great a debt we owe to those who went before us through the blood and sufferings of the Revolution.

—Sullivan Ballou, Civil War soldier from Rhode Island

Let us show the world a few more examples of men standing upon their own merit, and rising in spite of opposition.
—Joel Barlow, diplomat, "Letter to Noah Webster"

The time is not at hand when we shall see whether America has virtue enough to be free or not.
—Josiah Bartlett, 4th governor of New Hampshire

All great and honorable actions are accompanied with great difficulties, and both must be enterprised and overcome with answerable courage.
—William Bradford, governor of Plymouth Colony

I am fully persuaded that I am worth inconceivably more to hang for than for any other purpose.
—John Brown, abolitionist, speech at trial for treason and insurrection

Boys, the old flag never touched the ground.
—William H. Carney, US Civil War soldier, after the Battle of Fort Wagner

The worst tyrants are those which establish themselves in our own breasts.
—William Ellery Channing, preacher and theologian, "Spiritual Freedom"

Don't expect to build up the weak
by pulling down the strong.
—Calvin Coolidge, 30th president
of the United States

While we read history we make history . . . Every real crisis of
human history is a pass of Thermopylae, and there is always a
Leonidas and his 300 to die in it, if they cannot conquer.
—George William Curtis, *The Call of Freedom*

It's just a turn—and freedom.
—Emily Dickinson, poet, locking her door

The cost of liberty is less than the price of repression.
—W. E. B. Du Bois, *John Brown*

One of the earliest institutions in every New England
community was a pair of stocks. The first public building
was a meeting-house, but often before any house of God
was builded, the devil got his restraining engine.
—Alice Morse Earle, historian

Here once embattled farmers stood,
And fired the shot heard round the world.
—Ralph Waldo Emerson, "Hymn Sung at the
Completion of the Battle Monument, July 4, 1837"

Rally round the flag, boys—
Give it to the breeze!
That's the banner that we bore
On the land and seas.
—James T. Fields, "The Stars and Stripes"

Revenge proves its own executioner.
—John Ford, film director

We must all hang together, or assuredly we shall all hang
separately.
—Benjamin Franklin, inventor, at the
signing of the Declaration of Independence

Any time, any time while I was a slave, if one minute's
freedom had been offered to me, and I had been told I must
die at the end of that minute, I would have taken it—just to
stand one minute on God's earth a free woman—I would.
—Elizabeth Freeman, plaintiff,
quoted in *Brom and Bett v. Ashley*

Something there is that doesn't love a wall.
—Robert Frost, "Mending Wall"

Don't fight forces, use them.
—Buckminster Fuller, inventor

With reasonable men, I will reason; with humane men I will plead; but to tyrants I will give no quarter, nor waste arguments where they will certainly be lost.

—William Lloyd Garrison, journalist

Unless someone like you
cares a whole awful lot,
nothing is going to get better.
It's not.

—Theodor Seuss Geisel, *The Lorax*

Power lies in reason, resolution, and truth. No matter how long the tyrant endures, he will be the loser at the end.

—Kahlil Gibran, *Your Thought and Mine*

Freedom means the right to be stupid.

—Penn Gillette, comedian

No one who sets out to make the world better should expect people to enjoy it, all history shows what happens to would-be-improvers.

—Charlotte Perkins Gilman, author and activist

The Republic needed to be passed through chastening, purifying fires of adversity and suffering: so these came and did their work and the verdure of a new national life springs greenly, luxuriantly, from their ashes.

—Horace Greeley, journalist, *Greeley on Lincoln*

I only regret that I have but one life to lose for my country.
—Nathan Hale, spy, last words

There is a heartfelt satisfaction in reflecting on our exertions for the public weal, which all the sufferings an enraged tyrant can inflict will never take away; which the ingratitude and reproaches of those whom we have saved from ruin cannot rob us of. The virtuous asserter of the rights of mankind merits a reward, which even a want of success in his endeavors to save his country, the heaviest misfortune which can befall a genuine patriot, cannot entirely prevent him from receiving.
—John Hancock, 1st and 3rd governor of Massachusetts, "Boston Massacre Oration"

For every man who lives without freedom, the rest of us must face the guilt.
—Lillian Hellman, *Watch on the Rhine*

I believe in compulsory cannibalism. If people were forced to eat what they killed, there would be no more wars.
—Abbie Hoffman, activist

I say to you in all sadness of conviction, that to think great thoughts you must be heroes as well as idealists.
—Oliver Wendell Holmes Jr., former associate justice of the US Supreme Court, *The Profession of the Law*

We are not insensible that when liberty is in danger, the liberty of complaining is dangerous; yet a man on a wreck was never denied the liberty of roaring as loud as he could, says Dean Swift. And we believe no good reason can be given why the colonies should not modestly and soberly inquire what right the Parliament of Great Britain have to tax them.

—Stephen Hopkins, former governor of Rhode Island
and signer of the Declaration of Independence,
The Rights of the Colonies Examined

It is the courage of believing in freedom, per se, rather than of trying to force everyone to *see* that you believe in it—the courage of the willingness to be reformed, rather than of reforming—the courage teaching that sacrifice is bravery and force, fear—the courage of righteous indignation, of stammering eloquence, of spiritual insight, a courage contracting or unfolding a philosophy as it grows—a courage that would make the impossible possible.

—Charles Ives, composer, *Essays Before a Sonata*

Man, biologically considered, and whatever else he may be into the bargain, is simply the most formidable of all the beasts of prey, and, indeed, the only one that preys systematically on his own species.

—William James, philosopher and
psychologist, in the *Atlantic Monthly*

What has made this nation great?
Not its heroes but its households.
—Sarah Orne Jewett, author

Mankind must put an end to war or war will put an end to
mankind.
—John F. Kennedy, 35th president of the
United States, speech to the United Nations

How do you ask a man to be the last man to die for a mistake?
—John Kerry, 68th secretary of state, "Testimony before
Senate Foreign Relations Committee, April 22, 1971,"
regarding the Vietnam War

Even paranoids have enemies.
—Henry Kissinger, 56th secretary of state

Democracy gives every man
The right to be his own oppressor.
—James Russell Lowell, *The Biglow Papers*

On a thousand small town New England greens,
the old white churches hold their air
of sparse, sincere rebellion; frayed flags
quilt the graveyards of the Grand Army of the Republic.
—Robert Lowell, "For the Union Dead"

We are as great as our belief in human liberty—no greater. And our belief in human liberty is only ours when it is larger than ourselves.

—Archibald MacLeish, *Now Let Us Address the Main Question: Bicentennial of What?*

We didn't land on Plymouth Rock. The Rock was landed on us.
—Malcolm X, minister and activist

Freedom to be oneself is all very well; the greater freedom is not to be oneself.

—James Merrill, *A Different Person: A Memoir*

All real arguments are murderous.

—Arthur Miller, playwright

You're going to bring out every last man, even if you have to carry them on your backs.

—Henry Mucci, World War II colonel, to his Rangers before rescuing the survivors of the Bataan Death March

There's no war that will end all wars.

—Haruki Murakami, *Kafka on the Shore*

The genius of liberty, invigorated in this younger world, hath arrayed itself for the battle—it hath gone forth—it hath originated opposition—its banners have been displayed—it hath enlisted its worthies—the struggle hath been arduous, but the event hath crowned us with success—over veteran foes we have been victorious—independence claps her wings—peace is restored, governments are formed—publick faith established—and we bid fair to become a great and a happy people . . .
    —Judith Sargent Murray, activist, "The Gleaner"

Your true Yankee is always reasonable—always—even at the moment of unsheathing his sword, or pulling a hair-trigger.
    —John Neal, *The Down Easters*

War lives on a terrible sacrifice of life, and waste of substance. Yet greater evils can befall a people than the sacrifice of either upon the tented field.
    —William Henry Noble, Civil War general

Taxation without representation is tyranny.
    —James Otis Jr., lawyer

We have met the enemy, and they are ours.
    —Oliver Hazard Perry, War of 1812 naval commander, dispatch announcing victory at the Battle of Lake Erie

I burst the tyrant bands, which held my sex in awe.
            —Deborah Sampson, Revolutionary War soldier

A warrior never quits.

                    —Jeff Serowik, hockey player

My freedom is a privilege which nothing else can equal.
            —Venture Smith, farmer, *A Narrative of the
            Life and Adventures of Venture, a Native
            of Africa, but Resident Above Sixty Years
            in the United States of America*

Tonight, the American flag floats from yonder hill, or Molly
Stark sleeps a widow!
            —John Stark, Revolutionary War major general,
            before the Battle of Bennington, August 17, 1777

How nice it would be to sit in the garden and imagine that
we are living in a world in which everything was as it ought
to be.
            —Wallace Stevens, "Letter to Robert Frost"

The mass of men lead lives of quiet desperation.
            —Henry David Thoreau, *Walden*

History is the unfolding of miscalculations.
> —Barbara Tuchman, historian,
> *Stilwell and the American Experience in China*

Courage is resistance to fear, mastery of fear—
not absence of fear. Except a creature be
part coward it is not a compliment to say it
is brave; it is merely a loose misapplication
of the word. Consider the flea!—incomparably
the bravest of all creatures of God,
if ignorance of fear were courage.
> —Mark Twain, *Pudd'nhead Wilson*

To say that war is madness is like saying that sex is madness:
true enough, from the standpoint of a stateless eunuch,
but merely a provocative epigram for those who must make
their arrangements in the world as given.
> —John Updike, *Self-Consciousness*

The Puritans nobly fled from a land of despotism to a land of
freedom, where they could not only enjoy their own religion,
but could prevent everybody else from enjoyin' his.
> —Artemus Ward (Charles Farrar Brown),
> *London Punch Letters*

Stain not the glory of your worthy ancestors; but like them resolve, never to part with your birthright; be wise in your deliberations, and determined in your exertions for the preservation of your liberties. Follow not the dictates of passion, but enlist yourselves under the sacred banner of reason; use every method in your power to secure your rights; at least prevent the curses of posterity from being heaped upon your memories.

—Joseph Warren, doctor,
"1772 Boston Massacre Oration"

God grants liberty only to those who love it, and are always ready to guard and defend it.

—Daniel Webster, former US senator from
Massachusetts, "Speech, June 3, 1834"

A pure democracy is generally a very bad government. It is often the most tyrannical government on earth; for a multitude is often rash, and will not hear reason.

—Noah Webster, lexicographer,
The Original Blue Back Speller

The prospect of laying a foundation of liberty and happiness for posterity and securing asylum for all who wish to enjoy those blessings is an object in my opinion sufficient to raise the mind above every misfortune.

—William Whipple, Revolutionary War general

We owe no allegiance; we bow to no throne;
Our ruler is law, and the law is our own.
　　　　—John Greenleaf Whittier,
　　　　"Song of the Vermonters"

We must always consider that we shall be as a city upon a
hill, the eyes of all people are upon us.
　　　　—John Winthrop, governor of the Massachusetts Bay
　　　　　　Colony, "A Model of Christian Charity"

We were beyond fences, away from the clash of town-
clocks, the clink of town-dollars, the hiss of town scandals.
As soon as one is fairly in camp and has begun to eat with
his fingers, he is free.
　　　　—Theodore Winthrop, *Life in the Open Air*

CHAPTER 4

Highlands and Islands

Quotes about the landscapes and seascapes of New England

Since the glaciers retreated 18,000 years ago, the scenery of New England has been an inspiration to its inhabitants. In some ways it's a big landscape—the long cable of the Connecticut River Valley, the crooked arm of Cape Cod, the high peaks of the White Mountains. "The hills, rock-ribbed, and ancient as the sun," as poet William Cullen Bryant described, "The vales stretching in pensive quietness between; the venerable woods— rivers that move in majesty, and the complaining brooks that make the meadows green; and, poured round all, Old Ocean's gray and melancholy waste." But our Yankee hearts also tend toward the small—to the tumbled rock walls around a green field, a clapboard cabin deep in the woods. To one tiny island off our coast, to one tiny church on a village green. There is something here, in the rocks and soil, in the water and wind, that moves us. It might be in the molecules of the granite and the trap rock, or in the bark of the white pines and the yellow birches. It is certainly in the little cities, the picture-perfect hamlets, and the ancient paths in-between. Place matters. And no one knows this better than the sons and daughters of New England.

* * *

The gods of the valley are not the gods of the hills, and you shall understand it.
—Ethan Allen, farmer and patriot

Hold your hands out over the earth as over a flame. To all who love her, who open to her the doors of their veins, she gives of her strength, sustaining them with her own measureless tremor of dark life.
—Henry Beston, *The Outermost House*

The air smells so strong of codfish
it makes one's nose run and one's eyes water.
—Elizabeth Bishop, "At the Fishhouses"

Right here at my feet is what I've come to think of as the trout pool paradox. . . . The trout pool is a place for solitary contemplation, for romantic love, for a sense of reconnection with lost wilderness. And yet paradoxically, the pristine trout pools of western Connecticut nurtured the most noisome and alienating developments of the American industrial revolution—factory towns, foundries, mass production, the modern armaments and aerospace industries.
—George Black, *The Trout Pool Paradox*

No matter how tightly the body may be chained to the wheel of daily duties, the spirit is free, if it so pleases, to cancel space and to bear itself away from noise and vexation into the secret places of the mountains.
—Frank Bolles, *At the North of Bearcamp Water*

The aroma of New England is a mix of mulchy leaves, the hearth, cider, and crisp, cold sea.
—L. M. Browning, *Fleeting Moments of Fierce Clarity*

Little drops of water,
Little grains of sand,
Make the mighty ocean
And the pleasant land.
—Julia Fletcher Carney, "Little Things"

The beauty of Maine is such that you can't really see it clearly while you live there. But now that I've moved away, with each return it all becomes almost hallucinatory: the dark blue water, the rocky coast with occasional flashes of white sand, the jasper stone beaches along the coast, the pine and fir forests somehow vivid in their stillness.

—Alexander Chee, "Acadia National Park: Maine's Bright Face"

Over the river and through the wood,
To grandfather's house we go;
The horse knows the way
To carry the sleigh,
Through the white and drifted snow.

—Lydia Maria Child, *Flowers for Children (Thanksgiving Day)*

If the cities are allowed to become unfit for human habitation, the ruination of the countryside will proceed apace.

—Donald S. Connery, *One American Town*

Vermont is my birthright. Here one gets close to nature, in the mountains, in the brooks, the waters which hurry to the sea; in the lakes, shining like silver in their green setting; fields tilled, not by machinery, but by the brain and hand of man. My folks are happy and contented. They belong to themselves, live within their incomes, and fear no man.

—Calvin Coolidge, 30th president of the United States, from *Calvin Coolidge: Man from Vermont*

The choice is not between two landscapes, one with and one without human influence; it is between two human ways of living, two ways of belonging to an ecosystem.
—William Cronon, *Changes in the Land: Indians, Colonists, and the Ecology of New England*

The Brain—is wider than the Sky—
For—put them side by side—
The one the other will contain
With ease—and You—beside.
—Emily Dickinson, "Poem no. 632"

We must rebuild functioning communities with closer ties to the land not just in nostalgic fantasy, not just in token preservation, but in substantial daily practice. We must reclaim the commons.
—Brian Donahue, *Reclaiming the Commons: Community Farms and Forests in a New England Town*

The passage through all the rocky galleries of the Pine Tree Coast culminates at Quoddy Bay in a masterpiece.
—Samuel Adams Drake, *The Pine-Tree Coast*

It tosses up our losses, the torn seine,
The shattered lobster pot, the broken oar
And the gear of foreign dead men. The sea has many voices
Many gods and many voices.
—T. S. Eliot, "The Dry Salvages"

If once you have slept on an island you'll never quite be the same.
—Rachel Field, "If Once You Have Slept on an Island"

Whose woods these are I think I know.
His house is in the village though;
He will not see me stopping here
To watch his woods fill up with snow.
—Robert Frost, "Stopping by Woods on a Snowy Evening"

I am a big lover of the environment. I actually come from Maine, which is pretty much all environment.
—Noah Gray-Cabey, actor and pianist

We live where we live for landscape and seasons, for the place of it, but also for the time of it, daily and historical time.
—Donald Hall, *Here at Eagle Pond*

Tis a rough land of earth, and stone and tree
Where breathes no castled lord or cabined slave;
Where thought, and tongues, and hands, are bold and free,
And friends will find a welcome, foes a grave;
And where none kneel, save when to Heaven they pray,
Nor even then, unless in their own way.
—Fitz-Greene Halleck, "Connecticut"

Thus, by tracking our footprints in the sand, we track our own nature in its wayward course, and steal a glance upon it, when it never dreams of being so observed
—Nathaniel Hawthorne, "Foot-Prints on the Sea-Shore"

The smallest twig leans clear against the sky.
> —Sophia Peabody Hawthorne, painter,
> on the window of the Old Manse

The land is still being left behind, even by those who occupy it.
> —John Hay, *The Undiscovered Country*

I loved those hills, I loved the flowers
That dashed with gems their sunny swells,
And oft I fondly dreamed for hours,
By streams within those mountain dells.
> —James Abraham Hillhouse, lawyer,
> "Memory of Home"

We were standing where there was a fine view of the harbor and its long stretches of shore all covered by the great army of the pointed firs, darkly cloaked and standing as if they waited to embark. As we looked far seaward among the outer islands, the trees seemed to march seaward still, going steadily over the heights and down to the water's edge.
> —Sarah Orne Jewett, *Country of the Pointed Firs*

I was raised to believe that New England is the best place on the planet.
> —Abigail Johnson, businesswoman,
> "Speech of New Englander of the Year"

Our lake is never just a lake. It is a mirror of moods and can change daily, often hourly, from a placid pond without a ripple to a snarling beast with waves eight feet high.

—Dorothy Kidney, *A Home in the Wilderness*

You can see the goldenrod, that most tenacious and pernicious and beauteous of all New England flora, bowing away from the wind like a great and silent congregation.

—Stephen King, *Salem's Lot*

Beyond the very furthest range, where the pines turn to a faint blue haze against the one solitary peak—a real mountain and not a hill—showed like a gigantic thumbnail pointing heavenward.

—Rudyard Kipling, "In Sight of Monadnock"

Our landscape is a garden writ large, a synergy of human and natural forces.

—David K. Leff, *The Last Undiscovered Place*

New England has a harsh climate, a barren soil, a rough and stormy coast, and yet we love it, even with a love passing that of dwellers in more favored regions.

—Henry Cabot Lodge, former US senator from Massachusetts

Ocean is more ancient than the mountains, and freighted with the memories and the dreams of Time.

—H. P. Lovecraft, "The White Ship"

New England—too close to home to give us a living likeness.
　　　—Robert Lowell, "New England and Further"

There are times when a man wants solitude,
and particularly is this so when he is
watching the endless undulation of the sea.
　　　—Dudley Cammett Lunt, lawyer,
*The Woods and the Sea: Wilderness and
Seacoast Adventures in the State of Maine*

To see the earth as it truly is, small and blue and beautiful
in that eternal silence where it floats, is to see ourselves
as riders on the earth together, brothers on that bright
loveliness in the eternal cold—brothers who know now they
are truly brothers.
　　　—Archibald MacLeish, author

If a community has good walking paths through fields and
forests, people will use them. The right environment is a far
better teacher than a heap of manifestos.
　　　—Howard Mansfield, *The Same Ax, Twice*

As we have seen, man has reacted upon organized and
inorganic nature, and thereby modified, if not determined,
the material structure of his earthly home.
　　　—George Perkins Marsh, diplomat and environmentalist,
Man and Nature

Human beings—any one of us, and our species as a whole—
are not all-important, not at the center of the world. That is
the one essential piece of information, the one great secret,
offered by any encounter with the woods or the mountains
or the ocean or any wilderness or chunk of nature or patch
of night sky.

—Bill McKibben, environmentalist,
The Age of Missing Information

Consider the subtleness of the sea; how its most dreaded
creatures glide under water, unapparent for the most part,
and treacherously hidden beneath the loveliest tints of
azure. . . . Consider all this; and then turn to this green,
gentle, and most docile earth; consider them both, the
sea and the land; and do you not find a strange analogy to
something in yourself?

—Herman Melville, *Moby-Dick*

The twins of Sea and Land
Up and about for hours—hues, cries, scents—
Had placed at eye level a single light
Croissant: the harbor glazed with warm pink light.

—James Merrill, *The Changing Light at Sandover*

I'm spoiled by the lack of traffic, the beauty all around me,
the night sky, the wildlife, and having more space and time
to think and be creative.

—Julie Moir Messervy, landscape architect, in *Vermont Life*

These are sounds the landscape has never heard:
a strange human language, axes and saws,
iron hammers pounding home iron nails.
The tromp of boots, the cough of musket-fire.
Sighing, the old-growth trees crash to the ground,
opening a blue vista. Distant sails
scud on the wind, silent as butterflies.

—Marilyn Nelson, "The Meeting House"

I love the smell of freshly cut grass. It takes me back to the
summers in Maine.

—Rachel Nichols, actress

It is a scientific fact that the occasional contemplation of
natural scenes of an impressive character, particularly if
this contemplation occurs in connection with relief from
ordinary cares, change of air and change of habits, is
favorable to the health and vigor of men.

—Frederick Law Olmsted, landscape architect

The sea hates a coward.

—Eugene O'Neill, *Mourning Becomes Electra*

There are few things as involuntary as a person's
identification with a landscape.

—Terry Osborne, *Sightlines: The View of a
Valley Through the Voice of Depression*

When I was a child growing up in Maine, one of my favorite things to do was to look for sand dollars on the seashores of Maine, because my parents told me it would bring me luck. But you know, these shells, they're hard to find. They're covered in sand. They're difficult to see.

—Sarah Parcak, archaeologist

Ours is a land culture. In fact, the land is the culture.

—Aurelius Piper (Big Eagle),
Golden Hill Paugussett chief

I feel that my little bit of New England, which I know and love so well, is reeking with poetic suggestion.

—Henry Ward Ranger, artist, *Landscape Painting*

We don't have plays and music and contact with sophisticated minds, and a round of social engagements. All we have are sun and wind and rain, and space in which to move and breathe. All we have are the forests, and the calm expanses of the lakes, and time to call our own. All we have are the hunting and fishing and the swimming, and each other.

—Louise Dickinson Rich,
We Took to the Woods

On that Italian hilltop, winter after winter, I have been almost insupportably homesick for Maine scenes and scents: for the fresh, fragrant sea breeze, compounded of the essences of cool damp sand and moist brown seaweed; for the keen perfume of dying sweet grass in the haying season; for the springtime odors of lilacs, mallow and young willow leaves; for a smooth gray beach at the mouth of a tide river, and the raucous screams of mackerel gulls above it, hunting sand-eels; for the scent of autumn leaves, the sound of a bird-dog ranging an alder swale, the thunder of a rising partridge; for a lamp-lit kitchen and the steamy, appetizing odor of baked beans and new bread.

—Kenneth Roberts, journalist, *Trending into Maine*

Landscapes are not just material objects, explicable by some chronology of events in combination with the local climate and soil, but are presences that matter in human lives; they are experienced not only visually and kinesthetically, but aesthetically and emotionally as well.

—Kent Ryden, *Landscape with Figures*

The graveyards of New England can be gay or sad, humorous or severe, bleak or beautiful, but they are always intensely interesting. The spiritual history of our first two hundred years is nowhere written down more clearly than in these slate and granite pages of the hillside, these neglected Americana of the open air.

—Odell Shepard, *The Harvest of a Quiet Eye*

New England waters are some of my favorite—they are some of the richest waters because they are temperate waters and nutrient-rich, and therefore provide food for so many animals, from giant whales to sharks to everything else.

—Brian Skerry, photographer

Oh that we might be left alone for hours, to watch the changes of the landscape and hear the secret voice and dread revelations of these magnificent mountains! There are thoughts, deep and holy, which float through one's mind, as, gazing down upon such a scene, one contrasts the smallness of man with the magnitude of God's works, and, in the weird silence contemplates the perishable of this world with the everlasting hills.

—Thomas Sedgwick Steele, *Canoe and Camera: A Two-Hundred Mile Tour Through the Maine Forests*

The most beautiful thing in the world is, of course, the world itself.

—Wallace Stevens, poet

Whoever own the real estate and its constituents, the explorer owns the landscape.

—John Stilgoe, historian and photographer, *Outside Lies Magic*

61

Now the first of December was covered with snow
and so was the turnpike from Stockbridge to Boston
Though the Berkshires seemed dreamlike on account of
    that frosting
with ten miles behind me and ten thousand more to go.
                    —James Taylor, singer and songwriter,
                                        "Sweet Baby James"

The greater the threat of the far away to the near-at-hand,
the more precious grows this green and pleasant foothold
on the earth. Each morning we breathe what the urban man
thinks of as "that wonderful vacation air." Here we have
found the simple, the good, the satisfying life—not for
everyone, perhaps, but certainly for us. No other time, no
other place would suit us better.
    —Edwin Way Teale, *A Naturalist Buys an Old Farm*

Again and again appears the rainbow with lovely colors
melting into each other and vanishing, to appear again at
the next upspringing of the spray. On the horizon the white
sails shine; and far and wide spreads the blue of the sea,
with nothing between you and the eastern continent across
its vast, calm plain.
    —Celia Thaxter, *Among the Isles of Shoals*

In wildness is the preservation of the world.
    —Henry David Thoreau, *Walking*

However tidy well-built walls might appear, most functioned originally as linear landfills built to hold nonbiodegradable agricultural waste.
—Robert Thorson, scientist and journalist, *Stone by Stone: The Magnificent History of New England's Stone Walls*

Land of my birth, mine early love!
Once more thine airs I breathe;
I see thy proud hills tower above,
Thy green vales sleep beneath.
Thy groves, thy rocks, thy murmuring rills,
all rise before mine eyes.
—Laura Hawley Thurston,
"The Green Hills of My Father-Land"

They came singly and in groups, in small companies and in larger bands; and rapidly homes and farms dotted the valley, villages were built, and in an amazingly short time the wilderness had been conquered and tamed and the Connecticut Valley became the garden spot, the very heart of all New England.
—A. Hyatt Verrill, inventor and editor,
The Heart of Old New England

All that we do is touched with ocean, and yet we remain on the shore of what we know.
—Richard Wilbur, poet

How unsearchable are the depth of the wisdom and power of God in separating from Europe, Asia, and Africa such a mighty vast continent as America is?

—Roger Williams, theologian and founder of Rhode Island, "Of the Sea"

I thought to live on an island was like living on a boat. Islands intrigue me. You can see the perimeters of your world. It's a microcosm.
—Jamie Wyeth, artist

CHAPTER 5

Quotes about economics, politics, and society

Perhaps no quotation is more succinct, or more powerful, than the New Hampshire motto, seen on license plates and repeated by millions: "Live free or die." It expresses one of the cores of Yankee thought—and in four words is at once a political, commercial, and social statement.

In New England, and probably everywhere else, these three topics are hopelessly intertwined. From the staunch Federalists of the Revolution and early 19th century, to the loyal Republican supporters of Abraham Lincoln and Teddy Roosevelt, to the Democratic strongholds of the 21st century, our politics have always been passionate. They have also always been intensely local, always come down to arguments overheard in the check-out line at Dunkin' Donuts or Stop & Shop. And the fact that money is part of the concern is no accident. As one of our New England presidents, Calvin Coolidge, said to a convention of newspaper editors in 1925, "The chief business of America is business." The realities of New England merchants steered the course of American economic thought for centuries, and today the abstract theories of analysts who graduate from our business schools do the same.

Our society grows from these two forces, from the democracy that levels us into equality, and the capitalism that spreads us out. A citizen stands up from a wooden bench to raise a voice in a town meeting about a local ordinance that will affect her business. An opportunity to speak, an opportunity to thrive. That's all we want. If only we could all agree on the best way to do it.

* * *

The first requirement of a statesman is that he be dull. That is not always easy to achieve.
—Dean Acheson, 51st secretary of state

The great vice of this New England people is their adoration of Mammon. And rooted as it is in the character, the tree has now attained immense luxuriance and bids fair to overshadow us all.
—Charles Francis Adams, diplomat, *Diary*, October 6, 1833

No one ever attains very eminent success by simply doing what is required of him.
—Charles Kendall Adams, historian

The happiness of society
is the end of government.
—John Adams, 2nd president of the
United States, *Thoughts on Government*

Individual liberty is individual power, and as the power of a community is a mass compounded of individual powers, the nation which enjoys the most freedom must necessarily be in proportion to its numbers the most powerful nation.
—John Quincy Adams, 6th president of the United States, "Letter to James Lloyd, October 1, 1822"

Politics, as a practice, whatever its professions, had always been the systematic organization of hatreds, and Massachusetts politics had been as harsh as the climate.
—Henry Adams, *The Education of Henry Adams*

What a man has honestly acquired is absolutely his own, which may be freely given, but cannot be taken from him without his consent.
—Samuel Adams, 4th governor of Massachusetts

I cannot afford to waste my time making money.
—Louis Agassiz, geologist

Money talks—the only conversation worth hearing when times are bad.

—Fred Allen, comedian, *Much Ado About Me*

The sober, second thought of the people shall be law.

—Fisher Ames, former member of the US House of Representatives from Massachusetts, "Speech at Massachusetts Convention, 1788"

Where there is money, there is fighting.

—Marian Anderson, singer

I do not demand equal pay for any women save those who do equal work in value. Scorn to be coddled by your employers; make them understand that you are in their service as workers, not as women.

—Susan B. Anthony, activist, *The Revolution*

So long as we have enough people in this country willing to fight for their rights, we'll be called a democracy.

—Roger Baldwin, founder of the American Civil Liberties Union

Money is in some respects like fire; it is a very excellent servant but a terrible master.

—P. T. Barnum, showman, *The Art of Money-Getting*

The American people are uncomfortable with government activities that do not take place in the open, subject to public scrutiny and review.
—Dennis C. Blair, 3rd US director of National Intelligence

New England has a strong tradition of localism. What is ordinarily called election day in most of the United States is called town meeting day in Vermont.
—Murray Bookchin, political philosopher

Authority without wisdom is like a heavy axe without an edge, fitter to bruise than polish.
—Anne Bradstreet, *Meditations Divine and Moral*

Publicity is justly commended as a remedy for social and industrial diseases. Sunlight is said to be the best of disinfectants; electric light is the most efficient policeman.
—Louis D. Brandeis, former associate justice of the US Supreme Court, *Other People's Money*

Universities should be safe havens where ruthless examination of realities will not be distorted by the aim to please or inhibited by the risk of displeasure.
—Kingman Brewster, 17th president of Yale University

The surest way to return to the people's business is to listen to the people themselves.

—Scott Brown, former US senator from Massachusetts

The Government is here to serve, but it cannot replace individual service. And shouldn't all of us who are public servants also set an example of service as private citizens? So, I want to ask all of you, and all the appointees in this administration, to do what so many of you already do: to reach out and lend a hand. Ours should be a nation characterized by conspicuous compassion, generosity that is overflowing and abundant.

—George H. W. Bush, 41st president of the United States, "Remarks to Members of the Senior Executive Service"

The recipe for success is a tried and true one here in Rhode Island—innovation, reform, public service.

—Donald Carcieri, 73rd governor of Rhode Island

Patchwork is good economy.

—Lydia Maria Child, *The American Frugal Housewife*

Education is what is left after all that has been learnt is forgotten.
—James B. Conant, 23rd president of Harvard University

When a great many people are unable to find work,
unemployment results.
—Calvin Coolidge, 30th president of the United States

Opinions about the future of society are political opinions.
—Malcolm Cowley, *Exile's Return*

To fulfill a dream, to be allowed to sweat over lonely labor,
to be given a chance to create, is the meat and potatoes of
life. The money is the gravy.
—Bette Davis, actress, *The Lonely Life*

Status-seeking has to be fought anew in every generation.
The dedicated life is the life worth living. You must give
with your whole heart.
—Annie Dillard, author

To be a poor man is hard, but to be a poor race in a land of
dollars is the very bottom of hardships.
—W. E. B. Du Bois, *The Souls of Black Folk*

Slow, by degrees, politic systems rise;
Age still refines them, and experience tries.
This, this alone consolidates, improves;
Their sinews strengthens; their defects removes.
—Timothy Dwight, 8th president of Yale College

In society, one doesn't tell the truth, one tells the exact opposite.

—Nelson Eddie, singer

When we become ignorant, vicious, idle, our liberties will be lost—we shall be fitted for slavery, and it will be an easy business to reduce us to obey one or more tyrants.

—Oliver Ellsworth, 3rd chief justice of the US Supreme Court

To be great is to be misunderstood.

—Ralph Waldo Emerson, *Self-Reliance*

Vermont is the only place in America where I ever hear thrift spoken of with respect.

—Dorothy Canfield Fisher, author

Man is wronged, not in London, New York, or Boston alone. Look around you here in Worcester, and see him sitting amidst the dust of his counting room, or behind the counter, his whole soul engaged in dollars and cents, until the Multiplication Table becomes his creed, his Pater noster, and his Decalogue.

—Abby Kelley Foster, reformer, "Address to National Woman's Rights Convention"

Remember that time is money.
>—Benjamin Franklin, inventor,
>*Advice to a Young Tradesman*

Half the world is composed of people who have something
to say and can't, and the other half who have nothing to say
and keep on saying it.
>—Robert Frost, poet

Economics is not an exact science.
>—John Kenneth Galbraith, economist,
>*The Age of Uncertainty*

You cannot possibly have a broader basis for any
government than that which includes all the people, with
all their rights in their hands, and with an equal power to
maintain their rights.
>—William Lloyd Garrison, journalist

Management is the capacity to handle multiple problems,
neutralize various constituencies, motivate personnel. . . .
Leadership, on the other hand, is an essentially moral act,
not—as in most management—an essentially protective act. It
is the assertion of a vision, not simply the exercise of a style.
>—A. Bartlett Giamatti, former Major League Baseball
>commissioner, 19th president of Yale University,
>"An Address to School Administrators, 1987"

There's a whining at the threshold—
There's a scratching at the floor—
To work! To work! In Heaven's name!
The wolf is at the door!
—Charlotte Perkins Gilman,
"The Wolf at the Door"

It's not enough to profess faith in the democratic process.
We must do something about it.
—Ella T. Grasso, 83rd governor of Connecticut

I think, like everybody else in New Hampshire, when I pull
up to fill up my car and I pay $50, I get upset. And I'm
wondering if these prices are legitimate.
—Judd Gregg, 76th governor of New Hampshire

Despise the glare of wealth. That people who pay greater
respect to a wealthy villain than to an honest, upright man
in poverty, almost deserve to be enslaved; they plainly show
that wealth, however it may be acquired, is, in their esteem,
to be preferred to virtue.
—John Hancock, 1st and 3rd governor of
Massachusetts, "Boston Massacre Oration"

Happiness in this world, when it comes, comes incidentally. Make it the object of pursuit, and it leads us a wild-goose chase, and is never attained. Follow some other object, and very possibly we may find that we have caught happiness without dreaming of it.

—Nathaniel Hawthorne, *The American Note-Books of Nathaniel Hawthorne*

It would be hard to define chaos better than as a world where children decide they don't want to live.

—Edward Hoagland, author

Money cannot buy happiness, but it buys the conditions for happiness: time, occasional freedom from constant worry, a moment of breath to plan for the future, and the ability to be generous.

—John Hodgman, comedian, *Vacationland: True Stories from Painful Beaches*

Taxes are what we pay for civilized society.

—Oliver Wendell Holmes Jr., former associate justice of the US Supreme Court, *Compania de Tabacos v. Collector*

The moral flabbiness born of the exclusive worship of the bitch-goddess SUCCESS. That—with the squalid cash interpretation put on the word success—is our national disease.
—William James, philosopher and psychologist, "Letter to H. G. Wells"

If a free society cannot help the many who are poor, it cannot save the few who are rich.
—John F. Kennedy, 35th president of the United States, Inaugural Address

About one-fifth of the people are against everything all the time.
—Robert F. Kennedy, 64th US attorney general, "Speech at the University of Pennsylvania"

We're really all of us bottomly broke. I haven't had time to work in weeks.
—Jack Kerouac, *On the Road*

We create our future, by well improving present opportunities: however few and small they be.
—Lewis Latimer, inventor

In this nation, leadership is dollars.
—Norman Lear, television producer

Puritanism, believing itself quick with the seed of religious liberty, laid, without knowing it, the egg of democracy.

—James Russell Lowell, *New England Two Centuries Ago*

If money can fix it, it's not a problem.

—Tom Magliozzi, radio host, *Car Talk*

Education is our only political safety. Outside of this ark all is deluge.

—Horace Mann, educator, in *The New Era*

When faced with economic uncertainty, people don't want freedom. When they can't see their economic future, they want the nanny state.

—John McLaughlin, political commentator

Bitter it is to be poor and bitter to be reviled.

—Herman Melville, *Journal*

Brothers, we must be one as the English are, or we shall all be destroyed. You know our fathers had plenty of deer and skins and our plains were full of game and turkeys, and our coves and rivers were full of fish. But, brothers, since these Englishmen have seized our country, they have cut down the grass with scythes, and the trees with axes. Their cows and horses eat up the grass, and their hogs spoil our bed of clams; and finally we shall starve to death.

—Miantunnomoh, Narragansett grand sachem, from a 1642 speech to Long Island Indians

Ambition can be a disease, and it feeds on itself.
—Rebecca Miller, author and filmmaker

Although he's regularly asked to do so, God does not take sides in American politics.
—George J. Mitchell, former US senator from Maine

Give us the luxuries of life, and we will dispense with its necessities.
—John Lothrop Motley, historian

Yankee wealth is the creation of human hands, not of nature.
—Diana Muir, historian

You have the God-given right to kick the government around—don't hesitate to do so.
—Edmund Muskie, former US senator from Maine

I'm afraid the poor Indians will never stand a good chance with the English . . .they have no money. Money is almighty now-a-days.
—Samson Occum, Mohegan missionary

You just have to go as far as you can go. Everyone works his way up.
—David Ortiz, first baseman for the Boston Red Sox

All politics is local.
—Thomas P. "Tip" O'Neill Jr., former Speaker of the
US House of Representatives

I was happy, but I am now in possession of knowledge that this is wrong. Happiness isn't so bad for a woman. She gets fatter, she gets older, she could lie down, nuzzling a regiment of men and little kids, she could just die of the pleasure. But men are different, they have to own money, or they have to be famous, or everybody on the block has to look up to them from the cellar stairs.
—Grace Paley, "An Interest in Life"

If the environment were a bank, it would have been saved by now.
—Bernie Sanders, US senator from Vermont

It's a very sobering feeling to be up in space and realize that one's safety factor was determined by the lowest bidder on a government contract.
—Alan Shepard, astronaut
and first American in space

The strength of a nation, especially of a republican nation, is in the intelligent and well-ordered homes of the people.
—Lydia Sigourney, *Letters to Young Ladies*

Widespread ignorance bordering on idiocy is our new national goal. . . . The ideal citizen of a politically corrupt state, such as the one we now have, is a gullible dolt unable to tell truth from bullshit. An educated, well-informed population, the kind that a functioning democracy requires, would be difficult to lie to, and could not be led by the nose by the various vested interests running amok in this country.

—Charles Simic, "Age of Ignorance"

I do not want to see the Republican party ride to political victory on the Four Horsemen of Calumny—fear, ignorance, bigotry and smear.

—Margaret Chase Smith, former US senator from Maine

In a politically diverse nation, only by finding that common ground can we achieve results for the common good.

—Olympia Snowe, former US senator from Maine

The ultimate goal is to be an interesting, useful, wholesome person. If you're successful on top of that, then you're way ahead of everybody.

—Martha Stewart, businesswoman and television host

The man is richest whose pleasures are the cheapest.

—Henry David Thoreau, *Journal*

I am not a politician, and my other habits are good, also.

—Artemus Ward (Charles Farrar Browne), "Fourth of July Oration"

Politics makes strange bed-fellows.

—Charles Dudley Warner,
My Summer in a Garden

I don't believe that we all should eat squirrels and craft our own doorknobs.

—Elizabeth Warren, US senator from Massachusetts

Liberty exists in proportion to wholesome restraint.

—Daniel Webster, former US senator from Massachusetts

The foundation of all free government and all social order must be laid in families and in the discipline of youth. Young persons must not only be furnished with knowledge, but they must be accustomed to subordination and subjected to the authority and influence of good principles. It will avail little that youths are made to understand truth and correct principles, unless they are accustomed to submit to be governed by them.

—Noah Webster, lexicographer, "Letter to
David McClure, October 25th, 1836"

The only way not to think about
money is to have a great deal of it.
—Edith Wharton, *The House of Mirth*

Politics doesn't matter, policy does. That's what I try to get through to them, to steer them to make their own decisions rather than have someone preach to them.

—Brian J. White, actor

Civil or federal liberty is the proper end and object of authority, and cannot exist without it; and it is a liberty to do that only which is good, just, and honest.
—John Winthrop, governor of the Massachusetts Bay Colony, *Journal*

CHAPTER 6

Snowbound Winters and Indian Summers

Quotes about the seasons and weather of New England

From the frozen wastes of the little Ice Age to the humid summers of today, the climate in New England has been a constant source of wonder, anger, and disagreement. After all, our relatively small area includes the most famous autumn in America, some of the worst weather in the world on top of Mount Washington, and a variety of unpredictable, changeable conditions that defy human imagination. In fact, Hartford's Mark Twain made a famous speech on this phenomenon, saying in part, "One of the brightest gems in the New England weather is the dazzling uncertainty of it." On another occasion, he wrote more pithily, "If you don't like the weather in New England, just wait a few minutes."

That very uncertainty leads not only to some dangerous and dreadful moments, but to wonderful surprises. The sudden Indian summer of October, the beautiful snowfall at Christmas, the single flower in the midst of March storms. A late summer day that seems to stretch on forever, fireworks lighting the mirrored waters of a mountain lake. Our climate can be a Romantic poem or a Gothic horror, can produce grouchy complaints or reverential nostalgia, but it will never, ever, make us yawn with boredom.

* * *

Christmas wouldn't be Christmas without any presents.
—Louisa May Alcott, *Little Women*

Maine's long and cold winters may help keep our State's population low, but our harsh climate also accounts for what is unique and valuable about our land and our people.
—Tom Allen, former member of the
US House of Representatives from Maine

The one great poem of New England is her Sunday.
—Henry Ward Beecher, minister,
Proverbs from Plymouth Pulpit

Always, from the very beginning, it was snowflakes that
fascinated me most. The farm folks, up in this north
country, dread the winter; but I was supremely happy,
from the day of the first snowfall—which usually came in
November—until the last one, which sometimes
came as late as May.
—Wilson "Snowflake" Bentley, photographer,
The American Magazine

It is now the middle of March, cold winds stream between
earth and the severe assurance of the sun, winter retreats,
and for a little season the whole vast world here seems as
empty as a shell.
—Henry Beston, *The Outermost House*

Two sounds of autumn are unmistakable . . . the hurrying
rustle of crisp leaves blown along the street . . . by a gusty
wind, and the gabble of a flock of migrating geese.
—Hal Borland, journalist

And for the season it was winter, and they that
know the winters of that country know them to
be sharp and violent, and subject to cruel and
fierce storms, dangerous to travel to known
places, much more to search an unknown coast.
—William Bradford, governor of Plymouth
Colony, *Of Plymouth Plantation*

If we had no winter, the spring would not be so pleasant; if we did not sometimes taste of adversity, prosperity would not be so welcome.

—Anne Bradstreet, *Meditations Divine and Moral*

When I left the state of Maine for college, I met my first really rich friends, and I discovered summer could be a verb.

—Alexander Chee, author

A little Madness in the Spring
Is Wholesome even for the King.

—Emily Dickinson, "Poem no. 1333"

Words about winter;
Pull you inside the cold;
But the sun's never brighter;
Than when it's shining off snow.

—Tanya Donnelly, "Clipped"

From the hour when the Puritan baby opened his eyes in bleak New England, he had a Spartan struggle for life.

—Alice Morse Earle, historian

Go out of the house to see the moon, 'tis mere tinsel, it will not please as when its light shines upon your necessary journey. The beauty that shimmers in the yellow afternoons of October, who ever could clutch it? Go forth to find it, and it is gone: 'tis only a mirage as you look from the windows of diligence.

—Ralph Waldo Emerson, *Nature*

Nothing gold can stay.

—Robert Frost, poet

A small and sinister snow seems to be coming down relentlessly at present. The radio says it is eventually going to be sleet and rain, but I don't think so; I think it is just going to go on and on, coming down, until the whole world . . . etc. It has that look.
—Edward Gorey, illustrator, *Floating Worlds: The Letters of Edward Gorey & Peter F. Neumeyer*

We must admit, spring is annoying, summer is not ours, autumn is best—and winter is New England's truest weather.
—Donald Hall, *Here at Eagle Pond*

I cannot endure to waste anything so precious as autumnal sunshine by staying in the house.
—Nathaniel Hawthorne, *Notebook*, Oct. 10, 1842

July is the season of beaches and a blue sea, and an azure sky with white sails along the horizon.
—Jean Hersey, *The Shape of a Year*

When the cold comes to New England it arrives in sheets of sleet and ice. In December, the wind wraps itself around bare trees and twists in between husbands and wives asleep in their beds. It shakes the shingles from the roofs and sifts through cracks in the plaster. The only green things left are the holly bushes and the old boxwood hedges in the village, and these are often painted white with snow. Chipmunks and weasels come to nest in basements and barns; owls find their way into attics. At night, the dark is blue and bluer still, as sapphire of night.

—Alice Hoffman, *Here on Earth*

Certainty generally is illusion, and repose is not the destiny of man.

—Oliver Wendell Holmes Jr., former associate justice
of the US Supreme Court, *The Path of the Law*

In dark, cold solitude of winter months . . . I thank the Lord for this opportunity for reflection.

—Winslow Homer, painter

On suns and skies and clouds of June,
And flowers of June together,
Ye cannot rival for one hour
October's bright blue weather.
—Helen Hunt Jackson,
"October's Bright Blue Weather"

Touches of color showed in the foliage, the clusters on the wild grapevines had begun to turn purple, and the waysides were aglow with goldenrod. Up and down the steep hills crept the roads with many a graceful curve; and staggering board fences, patched and weather-stained and lichened, separated the highways from the scrubby pastures and irregular tracts of mowing-land.
—Clifton Johnson, *Highways and Byways of New England*

Here in purgatory bare ground
is visible, except in shady places
where snow prevails.
—Jane Kenyon, "Mud Season"

And what does the rain say at night in a small town, what does the rain have to say? Who walks beneath dripping melancholy branches listening to the rain? Who is there in the rain's million-needled blurring splash, listening to the grave music of the rain at night, September rain, September rain, so dark and soft? Who is there listening to steady level roaring rain all around, brooding and listening and waiting, in the rain-washed, rain-twinkled dark of night?
—Jack Kerouac, *The Town and the City*

Anyone who lives in Boston knows that it's March that's the cruelest, holding out a few days of false hope and then gleefully hitting you with the s@#t.
—Stephen King, *Dreamcatcher*

Here we become angry at an overcast day and accept God's light as though it were in the nature of things—as indeed I am beginning to believe that it is. The special beauty of the weather is that one can work largely, longly and continuously and the burden of the work evaporates in the sunshine so that a man can do much and yet not feel that he is doing anything.
—Rudyard Kipling, author, on his years in Vermont

The most serious charge which can be brought against New England is not Puritanism but February.
—Joseph Wood Krutch, *The Twelve Seasons*

One of the reasons we live in Vermont is that we love the cycle of the seasons—the contrast between hot and cold, wet and dry, wind and calm. The suspense that each day's and each hour's weather brings, keeps us guessing. We even get used to the idea that the weather is in fact, not predictable. It always gives us something to talk about. What do people talk about, I've often wondered, in parts of the country where the temperature is steady and the sun shines every day?
—Madeleine M. Kunin, "Gray Days of November"

One reason a lot of us live here is probably that surviving and flourishing in this climate is such a good, moral thing to do. It's decadent to be warm all the time.
—Willem Lange, *Tales from the Edge of the Woods*

New England has a harsh climate, a barren soil, a rough and stormy coast, and yet we love it, even with a love passing that of dwellers in more favored regions.
—Henry Cabot Lodge, former US senator from Massachusetts

The lowest ebb is the turn of the tide.
—Henry Wadsworth Longfellow, "Loss and Gain"

Spring has many American faces. There are cities where it will come and go in a day and counties where it hangs around and never quite gets there. Summer is drawn blinds in Louisiana, long winds in Wyoming, shade of elms and maples in New England.
—Archibald MacLeish, poet

By heaven, man, we are turned round and round in this world, like yonder windlass, and Fate is the handspike.
—Herman Melville, *Moby-Dick*

There are no ordinary seasons in New England, only years that are unusually rainy, or abnormally hot, or remarkably cold.
—Diana Muir, historian, *Reflections in Bullough's Pond: Economy and Ecosystem in New England*

In the Boston area every summer there are a few days so unpleasant you feel like cursing everything in sight.
—Haruki Murakami, *What I Talk About When I Talk About Running*

Both our traditional relationship to the land and the land itself have become distant. Yet spring speaks to each of us, in language our bodies first, then our minds, understand.
—Marilyn Nelson, "First Skunk of Spring," in *Black Nature*

The wheat has Spring in it.
—Gunilla Norris, *Becoming Bread*

A hot day,
a clear heaven—then
clouds bulge
over the horizon

and the wind turns
like a hundred black swans
and the first faint noise
begins.
—Mary Oliver, "Storm in Massachusetts,
September 1982"

Our New England climate is mild and equable compared with that of the Platte.
—Francis Parkman, historian, *The Oregon Trail*

In the same way that serious cold seems to invoke a new set of physical laws—altering the way sound carries, making the air less elastic—the coloring of maples and hickories and oaks overturns laws of space and light that have been in force since spring.

—Michael Pollan, *Second Nature: A Gardener's Education*

I guess no true Bostonian would trust a place that was sunny and pleasant all the time. But a gritty, perpetually cold and gloomy neighborhood? Throw in a couple of Dunkin' Donuts locations, and I'm right at home.

—Rick Riordan, *The Sword of Summer*

Do not speak with too much scorn of a wintry landscape. The wreaths of smoke rising high into the clear, blue skies, the pure, white covering under which nature reposes, the sparkling of the sinuous streams, where the graceful skaters glide, the groups of children, gathering rosier cheeks and merrier spirits from the heightened oxygen of the atmosphere, give to a winter morning in our sunny latitude cheering excitement.

—Lydia Sigourney, "The Pleasures of Winter"

Maine is a joy in the summer. But the soul of Maine is more apparent in the winter.

—Paul Theroux, "The Wicked Coast," *The Atlantic*

Gradually from week to week the character
of each tree came out, and it admired itself
reflected in the smooth mirror of the lake.
Each morning the manager of this gallery
substituted some new picture, distinguished
by more brilliant or harmonious coloring,
for the old upon the walls.
—Henry David Thoreau, *Walden*

There is a sumptuous variety about the New England weather that compels the stranger's admiration—and regret. The weather is always doing something there; always attending strictly to business; always getting up new designs and trying them on people to see how they will go. But it gets through more business in spring than in any other season. In the spring I have counted one hundred and thirty-six different kinds of weather inside of twenty-four hours.

—Mark Twain, *New England Weather*, speech to the New England Society, December 22, 1876

one minute a slender pine indistinguishable from the others
the next its trunk horizontal still green the jagged stump
a nest for the flickers

—Ellen Bryant Voigt, "Storm"

Everybody talks about the weather but nobody does anything about it.

—Charles Dudley Warner, author

The blast that swept him came off New Hampshire snow-fields and ice-hung forests. It seemed to have traversed interminable leagues of frozen silence, filling them with the same cold roar and sharpening its edge against the same bitter black-and-white landscape.

—Edith Wharton, "The Triumph of the Night"

When fall comes to New England
And the wind blows off the sea
Swallows fly in a perfect sky
And the world was meant to be.

—Cheryl Wheeler, "When Fall Comes to New England"

Here in New England, each season carries a hundred foreshadowings of the season that is to follow—which is one of the things I love about it. Winter is rough and long, but spring lies all round about.

—E. B. White, "Home-Coming"

When summer gathers up her robes of glory, and like a dream of beauty glides away.

—Sarah Helen Whitman, from "Poems"

Methinks I see the sunset light flooding the river valley, the western hills stretching to the horizon, overhung with trees gorgeous and glowing with the tints of autumn— a mighty flower garden blossoming under the spell of the enchanter, frost.
—John Greenleaf Whittier, *Tales and Sketches*

I prefer winter and fall, when you feel the bone structure of the landscape. Something waits beneath it; the whole story doesn't show.
—Andrew Wyeth, painter

CHAPTER 7

Competitions and Creations

Quotes about the sports, food, and culture of New England

So much of New England's culture became the culture of America that it is difficult to talk about it as an independent phenomenon. Our writers have certainly contributed more than their share to American literature, and we have supplied a lion's share to the creation of sports like football and basketball. Most quintessentially American foods have come from our kitchens, and quintessentially American images have come from our painters. So, when we talk about culture, what we are really talking about is our contribution to civilization, which exists not only in laws and government, roads and houses, but in novels, wine, and music. It is in the clatter of candlepin bowling and the roar of the crowd at a Patriots game. The taste of the first summer lobster roll and the swish of the first summer dress.

The heart of culture is a feeling—a togetherness, a solitude, a deep-in-your-bones reaction. And it is that feeling that makes us human. "Beauty is whatever gives joys," said poet Edna St. Vincent Millay, and there is abundant beauty in the creations and triumphs of civilization.

*   *   *

Here [in taverns] diseases, vicious habits, bastards, and legislators are frequently begotten.
—Samuel Adams, 4th governor of Massachusetts

Boozing does not necessarily have to go hand in hand with being a writer . . . I therefore solemnly declare to all young men trying to become writers that they do not actually have to become drunkards first.
—Nelson W. Aldrich, politician

I don't think violence on film breeds violence in life. Violence in life breeds violence in films.
—Robert Aldrich, film director, writer, producer

Even a fool knows you can't touch the stars, but it won't keep the wise from trying.

—Harry Anderson, actor and magician

Bottom line, you're either a risk taker, or you're not, and if you don't take risks, you'll never win big.

—Geno Auriemma, coach of University
of Connecticut women's basketball

My father loved thee through his length of days;
For thee his fields were shaded o'er with maize;
From thee what health, what vigor he possessed,
Ten sturdy freemen from his loins attest;
Thy constellation ruled my natal morn,
And all my bones were made of Indian corn.

—Joel Barlow, diplomat, "Hasty Pudding"

Music can name the unnameable and communicate the unknowable.

—Leonard Bernstein, conductor

The true competitors, though, are the ones who always play to win.

—Tom Brady, quarterback of the New England Patriots

I won 1,000 trophies, but sooner or later they all turn black.
—Ellison Myers Brown, two-time
winner of the Boston Marathon

Jazz stands for freedom. It's supposed to be the voice of freedom: Get out there and improvise, and take chances, and don't be a perfectionist—leave that to the classical musicians.
—Dave Brubeck, musician

In a sense I've made the same film over and over again. In all of them I've asked, Who are we as Americans?
—Ken Burns, filmmaker

An American athlete, when thirsty, ought to have only one drink—water.
—Walter Camp, father of American football

Usually, one's cooking is better than one thinks it is.
—Julia Child, chef and television host

Beauty is not caused. It is.
—Emily Dickinson, poet

Character is higher than intellect.
—Ralph Waldo Emerson, *The American Scholar*

If the human body recognized agony and frustration, people would never run marathons, have babies, or play baseball.

—Carlton Fisk, former catcher for the Boston Red Sox

Beer is proof that God loves us and wants us to be happy.

—Benjamin Franklin, author and inventor

Let it not be said, wherever there is energy or creative genius, 'She has a masculine mind.'

—Margaret Fuller, *Woman in the Nineteenth Century*

Win as though you were used to it, and lose as if you like it.

—Isabella Stewart Gardner, philanthropist

[Baseball] is designed to break your heart. The game begins in the spring, when everything else begins again, and it blossoms in the summer, filling the afternoons and evenings . . . it stops and leaves you to face the fall alone.

—A. Bartlett Giamatti, former Major League Baseball commissioner, 19th president of Yale University

I now live in the town of Concord, Massachusetts, not far from the Old North Bridge, where the American Revolution began. Whenever I take visitors to see the monument, and stand before the marble shaft, reading that lovely inscription which commemorates 'the shot heard round the world,' I think privately of Bobby Thompson's home run.

—Doris Kearns Goodwin, historian,
Wait Till Next Year: A Memoir

Creative ideas do not spring from groups. They spring from individuals. The divine spark leaps from the finger of God to the finger of Adam.

—A. Whitney Griswold, 16th president of Yale University

Together let us desire, conceive, and create the new structure of the future, which will embrace architecture and sculpture and painting in one unity and which will one day rise toward heaven from the hands of million workers like the crystal symbol of a new faith.

—Walter Gropius, architect, "The Bauhaus Proclamation April 1919"

Art, to me, is the interpretation of the impression which nature makes upon the eye and brain.

—Childe Hassam, painter

David Ortiz is a genius. He's incredible to watch. Over and over, he hits home runs that are simply transcendent.

—Juliana Hatfield, singer and songwriter

There are only two colors to paint a boat, black or white, and only a fool would paint a boat black.

—Nathanael G. Herreshoff, naval architect

What they call talent is nothing but the capacity for doing continuous work in the right way.

—Winslow Homer, painter

A nation's art is greatest when it most
reflects the character of its people.
—Edward Hopper, painter

Originality is the discovery of how to shed identity before
the magic mirror of Antiquity's sovereign power.
—Susan Howe, *My Emily Dickinson*

I not only blessed baseball, I was grateful for golf, thankful
for tennis, ecstatic for aquatics—for all those many health-
giving, body and character-building warm-weather pursuits
that keep our people in tone, and out of trout streams.
—William Humphrey, *My Moby Dick*

The word "beauty" is as easy to use as the word "degenerate."
Both come in handy when one does or does not agree with you.
—Charles Ives, composer, *Essays Before a Sonata*

Architecture is the art of how to waste space.
—Philip Johnson, architect

Sometimes it is necessary
To reteach a thing its loveliness.
—Galway Kinnell, "St. Francis and the Sow"

Bring on the heat because you can't beat us.
—Steve Kornacki, broadcast journalist, on the Patriots

Hang out with good people, do good things, and always put the team first.

—Robert Kraft, owner of the New England Patriots

Anything made with love, bam!—it's a beautiful meal.

—Emeril Lagasse, chef and television host

Nobody who ever creates anything of any importance ever does it without the help and inspiration of others.

—Bun Lai, chef

You don't always need stars to win. You don't always need greatness. Sometimes spirit, determination, fight will do as well.

—Napolean "Nap" Lajoie, second baseman in the Baseball Hall of Fame

An essential aspect of creativity is not being afraid to fail.

—Edwin Herbert Land, founder of Polaroid

Art is the objectification of feeling, and the subjectification of nature.

—Susanne K. Langer, philosopher and educator, *Mind: An Essay on Human Feeling*

When cerebral processes enter into sports, you start screwing up. It's like the Constitution, which says separate church and state. You have to separate mind and body.
—Bill Lee, former pitcher for the Boston Red Sox

Ideas can be works of art; they are in a chain of development that may eventually find some form.
—Sol LeWitt, artist

All books are either dreams or swords,
You can cut, or you can drug, with words.
—Amy Lowell, "Sword Blades and Poppy Seed"

Humanity is the keystone that holds nations and men together. When that collapses, the whole structure crumbles. This is as true of baseball teams as any other pursuit in life.
—Connie Mack, manager in the Baseball Hall of Fame

Culture is worth a little risk.
—Norman Mailer, author

Why waltz with a guy for 10 rounds if you can knock him out in one?
—Rocky Marciano, boxer

Real success is finding your lifework in the work
that you love.
—David McCullough, historian

A good newspaper, I suppose, is a nation talking to itself.
—Arthur Miller, playwright

Sport is born clean and it would stay that way if it was the
athletes who ran it for the pleasure of taking part, but then
the fans and the media intervene and finish up by corrupting
it with the pressure that they exercise.
—Bode Miller, skier

Photography is essentially a personal matter—a search for
inner truth.
—Inge Morath, photographer

And there ain't much to ice fishing till you miss a day or more
And the hole you cut freezes over
and it's like you have never been there before.
—Bill Morrissey, "Ice Fishing"

The invention of basketball was not an accident. It was
developed to meet a need. Those boys simply would not
play "Drop the Handkerchief."
—James Naismith, inventor of basketball, on his time at
Springfield College

When the time of year comes round with sap rising and snow melting, there is an insistent urge to take one's part in the process—to tap the trees, to gather the sap, to boil out the sweet syrup of the maple.
—Scott and Helen Nearing, *The Maple Sugar Book*

I'm from Maine. I eat apple pie for breakfast.
—Rachel Nichols, actress

Service must precede art. So long as considerations of utility are neglected or overridden by considerations of ornament, there will not be true art.
—Frederick Law Olmsted, landscape architect

Unfortunate combination of heterogeneous circumstances compelled us to succumb to the simultaneous and united endeavors of our opponents.
—Jim O'Rourke, outfielder in the Baseball Hall of Fame

I just love the feeling from the fans and when I'm walking on deck I can hear people screaming and wishing you the best. That puts you into the game more than anything.
—David Ortiz, former first baseman for the Boston Red Sox

You can't escape the taste of the food you had as a child. In times of stress, what do you dream about? Your mother's clam chowder. It's security, comfort. It brings you home.
—Jacques Pepin, chef and television host

You are what what you eat eats.
—Michael Pollan, *In Defense of Food: An Eater's Manifesto*

Language can inspire national pride, spirituality, and the freedom of the artistic soul.
—Bessy Reyna, poet

Most local cooks have two ideas about what to do with food. They either fry it, or else they make chowder out of it.
—Louise Dickinson Rich,
We Took to the Woods

Rock and Roll: Music for the neck downwards.
—Keith Richards, guitarist and songwriter

Without thinking too much about it in specific terms, I was showing the America I knew and observed to others who might not have noticed. My fundamental purpose is to interpret the typical American. I am a storyteller.
—Norman Rockwell, painter

I looked out this morning and the sun was gone
Turned on some music to start my day
I lost myself in a familiar song
I closed my eyes and I slipped away
                    —Tom Scholz, guitarist and songwriter,
                            "More Than a Feeling"

I enjoy the last quarter of all basketball games.
                            —Sarah Silverman, comedian

The world, and the fashion thereof, is so variable, that old
people cannot accommodate themselves to the various
changes and fashions which daily occur; *they* will adhere
to the fashion of *their* day, and will not surrender their
attachments to the *good old way*—while the young and the
gay, bend and conform readily to the taste of the times, and
fancy of the hour.
                            —Amelia Simmons, *American Cookery*

Paint what you see and look with your own eyes.
                            —Gilbert Stuart, artist

A great book should leave you with many experiences,
and slightly exhausted. You should live several lives while
reading it.
                            —William Styron, author

Sometimes the greatest enemy we compete against
during competition is not our opponent, but the thoughts
bouncing around in our own mind.

—Bob Tewksbury, former Major League
Baseball pitcher and psychologist

Oh! somewhere in this favored land the sun is shining bright;
The band is playing somewhere, and somewhere hearts are
light,
And somewhere men are laughing, and somewhere children
shout;
But there is no joy in Mudville—mighty Casey has struck out.

—Ernest L. Thayer, "Casey at the Bat"

Beware of all enterprises that require new clothes.

—Henry David Thoreau, *Walden*

If everyone did eat better, the world would be a better place.

—Ming Tsai, chef and television host

Work consists of whatever a body is obliged to do. . . . Play
consists of whatever a body is not obliged to do.

—Mark Twain, *The Adventures of Tom Sawyer*

The refusal to rest content, the willingness to risk excess on
behalf of one's obsessions, is what distinguishes artists from
entertainers, and what makes some artists adventurers on
behalf of us all.

—John Updike, author

Creating expands your soul.

—Kurt Vonnegut, author

Music acts like a magic key, to which
the most tightly closed heart opens.

—Maria Augusta von Trapp, singer

Language is the expression of ideas, and if the people of
one country cannot preserve an identity of ideas they cannot
retain an identity of language.

—Noah Webster, lexicographer, preface to
American Dictionary of the English Language

There are two ways of spreading light: to be the candle or
the mirror that reflects it.

—Edith Wharton, author

New York is great, but the New England fans are probably the
most knowledgeable and ardent fans, and not just in baseball,
but all sports. But Red Sox Nation is Red Sox Nation.

—Dick Williams, former manager of the Boston Red Sox

Baseball is the only field of endeavor where a man can
succeed three times out of ten and be considered a good
performer.

—Ted Williams, former outfielder for the Boston Red Sox

Our corn did prove well, and God be praised, we had a good increase of Indian corn, and our barley indifferent good, but our peas not worth the gathering, for we feared they were too late sown, they came up very well, and blossomed, but the sun parched them in the blossom; our harvest being gotten in, our Governor sent four men on fowling, that so we might after a more special manner rejoice together, after we had gathered the fruit of our labors; they four in one day killed as much fowl, as with a little help beside, served the company almost a week, at which time amongst other recreations, we exercised our arms, many of the Indians coming amongst us, and among the rest their greatest King Massasoit, with some ninety men, whom for three days we entertained and feasted, and they went out and killed five deer, which they brought to the plantation and bestowed on our Governor, and upon the captain, and others.

—Edward Winslow, governor of Plymouth
Colony, "Letter to Friends, 1621"

I find the earliest years of my life are
the source of my best inspiration.
—N. C. Wyeth, artist

CHAPTER 8

Rights and Justice

Quotes about struggles for a better world

In one of the most important statements ever made about human progress, Reverend Theodore Parker wrote, "The arc of the moral universe is long, but it bends toward justice." The United States was founded during a heroic bending of that arc, and ever since then, Americans of all races, genders, and creeds have tried to bend it further.

Often it doesn't want to bend. Sometimes fortune is unkind and people are unkinder. Sometimes our expectations are too high, or our hopes are greater than our abilities. As the old New England proverb goes, "Wishing isn't doing." But wishing leads to words. Words lead to action. Justice might be for the next world, but there have always been plenty of New Englanders trying to make it count in this one.

* * *

I wish most sincerely there was not a Slave in the province. It always appeared a most iniquitous Scheme to me—fight ourselves for what we are daily robbing and plundering from those who have as good a right to freedom as we have. You know my mind upon this Subject.

—Abigail Adams, patriot, "Letter to
John Adams, September 22, 1774"

All men are born free and equal, and have certain natural, essential, and unalienable rights.

—John Adams, 2nd president of the United States,
"Constitution of Massachusetts, June 15, 1780"

My toast would be, may our country be always successful, but whether successful or otherwise, always right.

—John Quincy Adams, 6th president of the
United States, "Address, July 4, 1821"

Political right and public happiness are different words for the same idea.

—Samuel Adams, 4th governor of Massachusetts,
"American Independence, August 1776"

I believe that it is as much a right and duty for women to do something with their lives as for men and we are not going to be satisfied with such frivolous parts as you give us.

—Louisa May Alcott, *Rose in Bloom*

No matter how big a nation is, it is no stronger than its weakest people, and as long as you keep a person down, some part of you has to be down there to hold him down, so it means you cannot soar as you might otherwise.

—Marian Anderson, singer

The true woman will not be exponent of another, or allow another to be such for her. She will be her own individual self,—do her own individual work—stand or fall by her own individual wisdom and strength . . . She will proclaim the "glad tidings of good news" to all women, that woman equally with man was made for her own individual happiness, to develop every power of her three fold-nature, to use, worthily every talent given to her by God, in the great work of life.

—Susan B. Anthony and Elizabeth Cady Stanton, "Statement, 1856"

Rights are . . . won only by those who make their voices heard.

—Roger Baldwin, founder of the American Civil Liberties Union

A human soul is not to be trifled with. It may inhabit the body of a Chinaman, a Turk, an Arab, or a Hotentot—it is still an immortal spirit!
—P. T. Barnum, showman, "Speech Supporting Universal Suffrage to the Connecticut House of Representatives"

The alternative is upon us; let us rather die freemen than live to be slaves. What is life without liberty?
—Ebenezer Bassett, diplomat, "Speech in Philadelphia, July 1863"

As long as a journalist tells the truth, in conscience and fairness, it is not his job to worry about consequences. The truth is never as dangerous as a lie in the long run. I truly believe the truth sets men free.
—Benjamin Bradlee, editor of the *Washington Post*

We may have democracy, or we may have wealth concentrated in the hands of a few, but we cannot have both.
—Louis D. Brandeis, former associate justice of the US Supreme Court

Intemperance and intolerance serve no one, and hatred guarantees failure.
—Edward Brooke, United States Senator from Massachusetts

There was a fire in the New England heart, in the intellectual depth of Calvinism, which the cold minds of Unitarian Cambridge possessed no knowledge of, a hunger for righteousness and a thirst for truth, a passionate dream of perfection.

—Van Wyck Brooks, *The Flowering of New England*

When I looked out the window, I saw my mother in an angry confrontation with the police. One of the officers lifted his billy club and hit her in the face with it. He busted her eye and she staggered back . . . I was deeply upset by what I had witnessed. I mean, I was only ten and I had just seen the police beat my mother in the face.

—Bobby Brown, singer, *Every Little Step*

All things are possible until they are proved impossible— and even the impossible may only be so, as of now.

—Pearl S. Buck, *A Bridge for Passing*

Healthy disagreement, debate, leading to compromise has always been the American way.

—Donald Carcieri, 73rd governor of Rhode Island

There are seasons, in human affairs, of inward and outward revolution, when new depths seem to be broken up in the soul, when new wants are unfolded in multitudes, and a new and undefined good is thirsted for. These are periods when . . . to dare is the highest wisdom.

—William Ellery Channing, preacher and theologian, *The Union*

I shall not live to see women vote, but I'll come and rap at the ballot box.

> —Lydia Maria Child, "Letter to Sarah Shaw, August 3, 1856"

We cannot do everything at once, but we can do something at once.

> —Calvin Coolidge, 30th president of the United States

Shall I be inactive and permit prejudice, the mother of abominations, to remain undisturbed? Or shall I venture to enlist in the ranks of those who with the Sword of Truth dare hold combat with prevailing iniquity?

> —Prudence Crandall, schoolteacher

Progress is a comfortable disease.

> —e. e. cummings, "no. 14"

When a man gives his opinion, he's a man. When a woman gives her opinion, she's a bitch.

> —Bette Davis, actress

The only thing that separates women of color from anyone else is opportunity.

> —Viola Davis, "Speech at the 67th Annual Emmy Awards"

Scientists search for truth. Philosophers search for morality. A criminal trial searches for only one result: proof beyond a reasonable doubt.

—Alan Dershowitz, lawyer

Every evil has its good, and every ill an antidote.

—Dorothea Dix, mental health activist

Liberty trains for liberty. Responsibility is the first step in responsibility.

—W. E. B. Du Bois, "John Brown"

Perfection is not the lot of human institutions.

—Oliver Ellsworth, 3rd chief justice
of the US Supreme Court

But what help from these fineries or pedantries? What help from thought? Life is not dialectics. We, I think, in these times, have had lessons enough of the futility of criticism. Our young people have thought and written much on labor and reform, and for all that they have written, neither the world nor themselves have got on a step. Intellectual tasting of life will not supersede muscular activity.

—Ralph Waldo Emerson, "Experience"

They that can give up essential liberty to obtain a little temporary safety deserve neither liberty nor safety.

—Benjamin Franklin, author, inventor

Sometimes duties act on the soul like weeds on a flower.
They crowd it out.

> —Mary E. Wilkins Freeman,
> "The Balking of Christopher"

There exists in the minds of men a tone of feeling toward
women as toward slaves.

> —Margaret Fuller, *Woman in the Nineteenth Century*

More die in the United States of too much food than
of too little.

> —John Kenneth Galbraith,
> economist, *The Affluent Society*

If you commence to talk about the superiority of men, if you
persist in telling us that after the fall of man we were put
under your feet and that we are intended to be subject to
your will, we cannot help you in New England one bit.

> —Eliza Ann Gardner, religious leader, "African Methodist
> Episcopal Zion Church Conference, 1884"

I will be as harsh as truth and as uncompromising as justice.
On this subject I do not wish to think, or speak, or write,
with moderation.

> —William Lloyd Garrison, journalist, *The Liberator*

I know up on top you are seeing great sights,
But down here on the bottom,
We too should have rights.
      —Theodor Seuss Geisel, *Yertle the Turtle*

Progress lies not in enhancing what is, but in advancing
toward what will be.
      —Kahlil Gibran, *A Handful of Sand on the Shore*

There is no female mind. The brain is not an organ of sex.
As well speak of a female liver.
      —Charlotte Perkins Gilman, *Women and Economics*

What I have done in this life has not been motivated by an
effort to save myself from unpleasant experiences in the next,
but rather, at least in part, by a desire to preserve the beauty
and biological integrity of the earth we have inherited.
      —Richard H. Goodwin, conservationist,
      A Botanist's Window on the Twentieth Century

Because I am a man.
      —Lewis Hayden, abolitionist and lecturer,
      on being asked why he wanted to be free

I put on pants fifty years ago and
declared a sort of middle road.
—Katharine Hepburn, actress

121

Society is always trying in some way or other to grind us down to a single flat surface.

—Oliver Wendell Holmes Sr.,
The Professor at the Breakfast Table

When will women begin to have the first glimmer that above all other loyalties is the loyalty to Truth, i.e., to yourself, that husband, children, friends, and country are nothing to that?

—Alice James, *Diary*

All the higher, more penetrating ideals are revolutionary. They present themselves far less in the guise of effects of past experience than in that of probable causes of future experience.

—William James, philosopher and psychologist,
The Will to Believe

The heresy of one age becomes the orthodoxy of the next.

—Helen Keller, disability rights activist, *Optimism*

Since I was a boy, I have known the joy of sailing the waters off Cape Cod. And for all my years in public life, I have believed that America must sail toward the shores of liberty and justice for all. There is no end to that journey, only the next great voyage. We know the future will outlast all of us, but I believe that all of us will live on in the future we make.

—Edward M. Kennedy, former
US senator from Massachusetts

Those who make peaceful revolution impossible will make violent revolution inevitable.
—John F. Kennedy, 35th president of the United States, "Address on the First Anniversary of Alliance for Progress"

Don't get mad, get even.
—Joseph P. Kennedy, diplomat

The final sin, the worst, is righteousness.
—Jack Kerouac, *The Dharma Bums*

A dream does not die on its own. A dream is vanquished by the choices ordinary people make about real things in their own lives . . .
—Jonathan Kozol, *Amazing Grace: The Lives of Children and the Conscience of a Nation*

Women who seek to be equal with men lack ambition.
—Timothy Leary, psychologist

The oldest and strongest emotion of mankind is fear, and the oldest and strongest kind of fear is fear of the unknown.
—H. P. Lovecraft, *Supernatural Horror in Literature*

Two wrongs don't never make a right.
—James Russell Lowell, *The Biglow Papers*

If you aren't careful, the newspapers will have you hating
the people who are being oppressed and loving the people
who are doing the oppressing.

—Malcolm X, minister and activist

Nothing which is worth while is easy, nor in my experience
is the actual doing of it particularly pleasant. The pleasure
arises from completion and from the knowledge that one
has done the right thing and has stood by one's convictions.

—John P. Marquand, *The Late George Apley*

Do enough; Do Good, Be Spurned, Do More Good.

—Cotton Mather, minister

It were better that Ten Suspected Witches should escape,
than that one Innocent Person should be Condemned.

—Increase Mather, *Cases of Conscience Concerning Evil
Spirits Personating Men, Witchcrafts, Infallible Proofs
of Guilt in Such as Are Accused with That Crime*

I have a vision of the world as a global village, a world
without boundaries.

—Christa McAuliffe, astronaut

I would calmly ask, is it reasonable, that a
candidate for immortality, for the joys of heaven,
an intelligent being, who is to spend an eternity
in contemplating the works of Deity, should
at present be so degraded, as to be allowed
no other ideas, than those suggested by the
mechanism of a pudding, or the sewing [of]
the seams of a garment?
—Judith Sargent Murray, activist,
On the Equality of the Sexes

The voice of protest, of warning, of appeal is never more
needed than when the clamor of fife and drum, echoed by
the press and too often by the pulpit, is bidding all men fall
in and keep step and obey in silence, the tyrannous word of
command. Then, more than ever, it is the duty of the good
citizen not to be silent.
—Charles Eliot Norton, "True Patriotism"

To some will come a time when change itself is beauty, if
not heaven.
—Edwin Arlington Robinson, poet

Sociology was born of the modern ardor to improve society.
—Albion Woodbury Small, sociologist,
An Introduction to the Study of Society

The right way is not always the popular and easy way. Standing for right when it is unpopular is a true test of moral character.

—Margaret Chase Smith, former US senator from Maine

Defend your ideas, but be flexible. Success seldom comes in exactly the form you imagine.

—Martha Stewart, businesswoman and television host

The right of conscience and private judgment is unalienable, and it is truly the interest of all mankind to unite themselves into one body for the liberty, free exercise, and unmolested enjoyment of this right.

—Ezra Stiles, 7th president of Yale College

We want rights. The flour merchant, the house-builder, and the postman charge us no less on account of our sex; but when we endeavor to earn money to pay all these, then, indeed, we find the interest.

—Lucy Stone, activist, National Woman's Rights Convention

I wrote what I did because as a woman, as a mother, I was oppressed and broken-hearted with the sorrows of injustice I saw.
—Harriet Beecher Stowe, on *Uncle Tom's Cabin*

Where Slavery is, there Liberty cannot be; and where Liberty is, there Slavery cannot be.
—Charles Sumner, former US senator from Massachusetts, *Slavery and the Rebellion*

I felt fighting discrimination was the most important thing I could do as an elected official. I said then and I believe now, that any doctrine of superiority is scientifically false, morally condemnable, socially unjust and dangerous.
—Gerald Talbot, civil and human rights advocate

Mr. President, shall it be said, that after we have established our own independence and freedom, we make slaves of others?
—Brigadier Samuel Thompson, Revolutionary War soldier, on the question of slavery and the Constitution

I know of no more encouraging fact than the unquestionable ability of man to elevate his life by a conscious endeavor.
—Henry David Thoreau, *Walden*

Justice, Sir, is the great interest of man on earth.
—Daniel Webster, former US senator from Massachusetts, "Oration on the Day of Justice Joseph Story's Funeral"

When a citizen gives his suffrage to a man of known immorality he abuses his trust; he sacrifices not only his own interest, but that of his neighbor; he betrays the interest of his country.

—Noah Webster, lexicographer, *Letters to a Young Gentleman Commencing His Education*

We have nothing to fear for the future, except as we shall forget the way the Lord has led us, and His teaching in our past history.
—Ellen G. White, co-founder of the Seventh-Day Adventist Church

Enforced uniformity confounds civil and religious liberty and denies the principles of Christianity and civility. No man shall be required to worship or maintain a worship against his will.

—Roger Williams, theologian and founder of Rhode Island

CHAPTER 9

Outside Looking In, Inside Looking Out

Quotes by visitors to New England, quotes by New Englanders about the rest of the world

Since the late 1600s New Englanders have traveled to and traded with all the nations of the globe, and they have had particular things to say about what they found. Likewise, our world-famous schools and colleges and our pleasant hills and shores have attracted many visitors, from Charles Dickens to the Marquis de Lafayette, and they also had very particular things to say about what they found here. New England is a part of the world, whether our grumpy, solitary souls like it or not, and we are subject to its opinions and criticisms.

Luckily, we get to do the same to everyone else. As Benjamin Botkin, author of *Treasury of New England Folklore*, put it, "To the rest of the country, New England has always stood in much the same relation as England has to America—that of spiritual homeland and mother country." And since in the past century American culture has permeated every corner of the world, our little land can be said to be a foundation of world civilization. Right?

Perhaps not. But you can be sure we will go on talking like it is. And the rest of the world will just as surely talk back.

* * *

I have just returned from Boston. It is the only thing to do if you find yourself up there.

—Fred Allen, comedian, "Letter to Groucho Marx, June 12, 1953"

All I know is that history repeats itself and people are going to want to experience the world. But I know then they are going to have a better appreciation for what is here in Maine.

—John Baldacci, 73rd governor of Maine

No! Not a bit of it! Why, sir, you can't imagine the
difference. There, everything is frozen—kings and things—
formal, but absolutely frozen, here it is life. Here it is
freedom, and here are men.

—P. T. Barnum, showman, on being
asked whether he preferred Europe

O beautiful for spacious skies,
For amber waves of grain,
For purple mountain majesties
Above the fruited plain!
America! America!
God shed His grace on thee,
And crown thy good with brotherhood
From sea to shining sea!

—Katharine Lee Bates,
"America the Beautiful"

I think almost the last straw here though is the hairdresser,
a nice big hearty Maine girl who asks me questions I don't
even know the answers to. She told me: One, that my
hair 'don't feel like hair at all.' Two, I was turning gray
practically 'under her eyes.' And when I'd said yes, I was an
orphan, she said 'Kind of awful, ain't it, ploughing through
life alone.' So now I can't walk downstairs in the morning or
upstairs at night without feeling like I'm ploughing. There's
no place like New England.

—Elizabeth Bishop, *Words in Air: The Complete
Correspondence Between Elizabeth Bishop
and Robert Lowell*

There are a few essential elements you find in the spirit of a Mainer; a humble appreciation of well-crafted things, wit dry enough you may not know when the joke ends and when it begins and most importantly, a love for the land and the sea.

—Anthony Bourdain, chef and television host

In New England there are three times of year. Either winter has just been, or winter is coming, or it's winter.

—Bill Bryson, *Notes from a Big Country*

What people can excel our Northern and New England brethren in skill, invention, activity, energy, perseverance, and enterprise?

—John C. Calhoun, former senator from South Carolina

I sing New England, as she lights her fire
In every Prairie's midst; and where the bright
Enchanting stars shine pure through Southern night,
She still is there, the guardian on the tower,
To open for the world a purer hour.

—William Ellery Channing, preacher
and theologian, *New England*

I always figured the American public wanted a solemn ass for President, so I went along with them.

—Calvin Coolidge, 30th president of the United States

And I've always heer'n say that the Bay State was provarbal
for pronounsation.

—James Fenimore Cooper, *The Pioneers*

The ever-raging ocean was all that presented itself to
the view of this family; it irresistibly attracted my whole
attention: my eyes were involuntarily directed to the
horizontal line of that watery surface, which is ever in
motion and ever threatening destruction to these shores.
My ears were stunned with the roar of its waves rolling
one over the other, as if impelled by a superious force to
overwhelm the spot on which I stood.

—J. Hector St. John Crevecoeur,
"Peculiar Customs at Nantucket"

We've got the long hair, we've got the cornrows,
we got just guys acting like idiots. And I think
the fans out there like it.
—Johnny Damon, former outfielder
for the Boston Red Sox

These towns and cities of New England (many of which
would be villages in Old England), are as favourable
specimens of rural America, as their people are of rural
Americans. The well-trimmed lawns and green meadows
of home are not there; and the grass, compared with our
ornamental plots and pastures, is rank, and rough, and

wild: but delicate slopes of land, gently-swelling hills, wooded valleys, and slender streams, abound. Every little colony of houses has its church and school-house peeping from among the white roofs and shady trees; every house is the whitest of the white; every Venetian blind the greenest of the green; every fine day's sky the bluest of the blue.

—Charles Dickens, *American Notes*

It is a peculiar sensation, this double-consciousness, this sense of always looking at one's self through the eyes of others, of measuring one's soul by the tape of a world that looks on in amused contempt and pity.

—W. E. B. Du Bois, *The Souls of Black Folk*

I cherish as strong a love for the land of my nativity as any man living. I am proud of her civil, political, and religious institutions—of her high advancement in science, literature and the arts—of her general prosperity and grandeur. But I have some solemn accusations to bring against her.

—William Lloyd Garrison, journalist

Political corruption is to Rhode Islanders as smog is to people who live in Los Angeles: nobody complains of its absence, but when it rolls around everyone feels right at home.

—Philip Gourevitch, in *The New Yorker*

I was raised as an upper-class WASP in New England, and there was this old tradition there that everyone would simply be guided into the right way after Ivy League college and onward and upward. And it rejected me, I rejected it, and I ended up as a kind of refugee, really.
—Spalding Gray, monologist

If any young man is about to commence the world, we say to him, publicly and privately, Go to the West.
—Horace Greeley, journalist

New York has people, the Northwest rain, Iowa soybeans, and Texas money. New Hampshire has weather and seasons.
—Donald Hall, *Here at Eagle Pond*

The Yankees see further ahead than most folks; they can even a most see round t'other side of a thing; indeed some on them have hurt their eyes by it, and sometimes I think that's the reason such a sight of them wear spectacles.
—Thomas Chandler Halliburton, *The Clockmaker*

It would be difficult to conceive of any more dogmatic and less tolerant people than the first settlers on New England shores.
—Paul Harris, entertainer

An American tree, however, if it could grow in fair competition with an English one of similar species, would probably be the more picturesque object of the two.
—Nathaniel Hawthorne, *Our Old Home*

I've lived in California, Africa, New Guinea, South America, and the High Arctic. But I've come back to the hills of western Maine. These are my favorite haunts, because this is home, where the subtle matters, and the spectacular distracts.
—Bernd Heinrich, *A Year in the Maine Woods*

Good Americans, when they die, go to Paris.
—Oliver Wendell Holmes Sr.,
The Autocrat of the Breakfast Table

Well I'm on the Downeaster "Alexa"
And I'm cruising through Block Island Sound,
I have charted a course to the Vineyard
But tonight I am Nantucket bound.
—Billy Joel, singer and songwriter,
"The Downeaster Alexa"

Those New England States, I do believe, will be the noblest country in the world in a little while. They will be the salvation of that very great body with a very little soul, the rest of the United States; they are the pith and marrow, heart and core, head and spirit of that country.
—Fanny Kemble, *A Year of Consolation*

From the prodigious hilltops of New Hampshire, let
freedom ring.
        —Martin Luther King Jr., minister and activist

It is with profound respect that I tread upon this hallowed
ground, where the blood of American patriots, the blood
of Warren and his companions, gloriously spilled, revived
the force of three million men and secured the happiness
of ten million who live now, and of so many others to be
born. This blood has summoned the American continents to
republican independence, and has awakened in the nations
of Europe the necessity of, and assured for the future, I
hope, the exercise of their rights.
        —Marquis de Lafayette, "Speech at the
            Bunker Hill Monument, 1824"

A sinking feeling that here is a transient, a tourist, a
caretaker, and not the householder; that men live in New
England as the Venetian now lives in Venice . . . All this
white and green and blue is precariously too perfect.
        —Robert Lowell, "New England and Further"

I believe no one attempts
to praise the climate of New England.
—Harriet Martineau,
Retrospect of Western Travel

I actually realized that I was somebody important, because I caught the attention of 60,000 people, plus you guys, plus the whole world watching a guy that if you reverse the time back fifteen years ago, I was sitting under a mango tree without fifty cents to actually pay for a bus. And today, I was the center of attention of the whole city of New York. I thank God for that, and you know what? I don't regret one bit what they do out there. I respect them, and I actually kind of like it because I don't like to brag about myself, I don't like to talk about myself, but they did make me feel important.

—Pedro Martinez, former pitcher for the
Boston Red Sox, on being booed in New York

Too green the springing April grass,
Too blue the silver-speckled sky,
For me to linger here, alas,
While happy winds go laughing by,
Wasting the golden hours indoors,
Washing windows and scrubbing floors.

—Claude McKay, "Spring in New Hampshire"

But appearances all the world over are deceptive.

—Herman Melville, *Typee*

I have lived more than half my life in the Connecticut countryside, all the time expecting to get some play or book finished so I can spend more time in the city, where everything is happening.

—Arthur Miller, *Timeshifts*

The men who founded and governed
Massachusetts and Connecticut took themselves
so seriously that they kept track of everything
they did for the benefit of posterity and hoarded
their papers so carefully that the whole history
of the United States, recounted mainly by their
descendants, has often appeared to be the
history of New England writ large.
—Edmund Morgan, historian

Your Excellency, Governor of the Commonwealth of
Massachusetts, without intending to depart from the
priorities of the occasion, it may be proper to say that
those of us who came from beyond the Hudson can but feel
that in entering New England we reach the birthplace of
American Institution.
—Lewis H. Morgan, anthropologist,
Address in Boston, August 26, 1880

The only thing we can do is work hard, and all the negativity
that's in this town sucks.
—Rick Pitino, former coach of the Boston Celtics

Oh, the ignorance of us upon whom Providence did not
sufficiently smile to permit us to be born in New England.
—Horace Porter, ambassador to France

New Englanders began the Revolution not to institute reforms and changes in the order of things, but to save the institutions and customs that already had become old and venerable with them; and were new only to a few stupid Englishmen a hundred and fifty years behind the times.

—Edward Pearson Pressey, *History of Montague: A Typical Puritan Town*

I'm tired of them. They're tired of me.

—Manny Ramirez, former outfielder for the Boston Red Sox, on being traded to the Los Angeles Dodgers

Vermont is a small state which makes an enormous difference.

—Fred Rogers, television host, Commencement Address at Middlebury College, May 2001

Did you ever see a place that looks like it was built just to enjoy? Well, this whole state of Maine looks that way to me.

—Will Rogers, entertainer

So when I reached my prime
I left my home in the Maritimes
Headed down the turnpike for
New England, sweet New England.

—Paul Simon, singer and songwriter, "Duncan"

You don't want someone to think you're from New Hampshire, because who cares about New Hampshire? You're basically just a pass-through.

—Timothy Simon, actor

The New England conscience doesn't keep you from doing what you shouldn't—it just keeps you from enjoying it.

—Isaac Bashevis Singer, author

If the people in Britain knew the nature and disposition of the New England people as well as we do they would not find so many friends in England as I suppose they do.

—Nathaniel Smith, former member of the
US House of Representatives from Connecticut

I looked along the San Juan Islands and the coast of California, but I couldn't find the palette of green, granite, and dark blue that you can only find in Maine.

—Parker Stevenson, actor

I have traveled over Europe but nowhere can you see the progress of this age so ingeniously shown as in America. The superiority of the new over the old country is shown in your press rooms, in your railroad carriages, and in fact in every branch of industry . . . no place suits me as well as America.

—Charles Stratton (General Tom Thumb), entertainer

In the kind of New England I'm from, you are expected to stay and marry somebody from New England—well, Maine, actually—so I think it was seen as a betrayal when I left for New York, which has been my refuge.

—Elizabeth Strout, author

Most people, when they imagine New England, think about old colonial homes, white houses with black shutters, whales, and sexually morbid WASPs with sensible vehicles and polite political opinions. This is incorrect. If you want to get New England right, just imagine a giant mullet in paint-stained pants and a Red Sox hat being pushed into the back of a cruiser after a bar fight.

—Matt Taibbi, journalist, *Spanking the Donkey: Dispatches from the Dumb Season*

I hadn't been in Vermont very long, but I'd been there long enough to know what any Vermonter worth his salt would think of [being on his property]. Trespassing on someone's land was tantamount to breaking into his house.

—Donna Tartt, *The Secret History*

The Yankee: In acuteness and perseverance, he resembles the Scotch. In frugal neatness, he resembles the Dutch. But in truth, a Yankee is nothing else on earth but himself.

—Frances Trollope, *Domestic Manners of the Americans*

Travel is fatal to prejudice, bigotry, and narrow-mindedness, and many of our people need it sorely on these accounts. Broad, wholesome, charitable views of men and things cannot be acquired by vegetating in one little corner of the earth all one's lifetime.

—Mark Twain, *The Innocents Abroad*

My idea of a republic is a little state in the north of your great country, one of the smallest of the New England states—Vermont . . . To be a son of Vermont is glory enough for the greatest citizen.

—Otto von Bismarck, 1st chancellor of the German Empire

The highest treason in the USA is to say Americans are not loved, no matter where they are, no matter what they are doing there.

—Kurt Vonnegut, *A Man Without a Country*

We learned the shocking truth that "home" isn't necessarily a certain spot on earth. It must be a place where you can "feel" at home, which means "free" to us.

—Maria Augusta von Trapp,
The Story of the Trapp Family Singers

We cannot and ought not wholly to divest ourselves of provincial views and attachments, but we should subordinate them to the general interests of the continent.

—Noah Webster, lexicographer,
Sketches of American Policy

I would really rather feel bad in Maine
than feel good anywhere else.
—E. B. White, author

We Americans have yet to really learn our own antecedents,
and sort them, to unify them. They will be found ampler
than has been supposed, and in widely different sources.
Thus far, impressed by New England writers and
schoolmasters, we tacitly abandon ourselves to the notion
that our United States has been fashion'd from the British
Islands only, and essentially form a second England only—
which is a very great mistake.

—Walt Whitman, "The Spanish Element
in Our Nationality"

Rhode Island was settled and is made up of people who
found it unbearable to live anywhere else in New England.

—Woodrow Wilson, 28th president of the
United States, January 29, 1911

CHAPTER 10

Happiness and Heartbreak

Quotes about relationships, family, and romance

Love can be a fragile thing, and marriage can sometimes seem to be the most impermanent of modern institutions. "How frail the human heart must be," said Sylvia Plath. "A mirrored pool of thought." Besides, the end of every love story is always dark. Everyone dies, and any happy story is a denial of that fact, a photograph rather than a film, an illusion rather than immortality. That is why tragic stories have more lasting permanence.

But even some reserved and skeptical New Englanders refuse to believe that. Or maybe they believe that this is only part of the truth. Who says that happiness needs permanence? There is a truth in the transitory, in the fleeting, that balances the other. There is one moment after the next, each enjoyed to its fullest, before the window shuts. As Thornton Wilder wrote in *The Bridge of San Luis Rey*, "There is a land of the living and a land of the dead, and the bridge is love, the only survival, the only meaning." It's a bridge we must try to build, together.

* * *

Virtue is not always amiable.
  —John Adams, 2nd president of the United States, *Diary*

Love is the only thing that we can carry with us when we go, and it makes the end so easy.
  —Louisa May Alcott, *Little Women*

Relations between the sexes are so complicated that the only way you can tell if two members of the set are "going together" is if they are married. Then, almost certainly, they are not.
  —Cleveland Amory, animal rights activist,
Who Killed Society

Marriage, to women as to men, must be a luxury, not a necessity; an incident of life, not all of it. And the only possible way to accomplish this great change is to accord to women equal power in the making, shaping and controlling of the circumstances of life.
  —Susan B. Anthony, activist, "Speech on Social Purity"

Love is the strongest emotion any creature can feel except for hate, but hate can't hurt you. Love, and trust, and friendship, and all the other emotions humans value so much, are the only emotions that can bring pain. Only love can break a heart into so many pieces.
—Amelia Atwater-Rhodes, *In the Forests of the Night*

The noblest art is that of making others happy.
—P. T. Barnum, showman, *Struggles and Triumphs*

If ever two were one, then surely we.
If ever man were loved by wife, then thee;
If ever wife was happy in a man,
Compare with me ye women if you can.
—Anne Bradstreet,
"To My Dear and Loving Husband"

Men and women should own the world as a mutual possession.
—Pearl S. Buck, *Of Men and Women*

Ain't nothin' gonna save you
From a love that's blind
You slip to the dark side
Across that line
—John Cafferty, "On the Dark Side"

We are the puzzle pieces who seldom fit with other puzzle pieces. Romantics, idealists, eccentrics, we inhabit single-dom as our natural resting state. In a world where proms and marriages define the social order, we are, by force of our personalities and inner strengths, rebels.

—Sasha Cagen, author

Be loyal to those who are loyal to you. And respect everyone, even your enemies and competition.

—John Cena, wrestler and actor

I think careful cooking is love, don't you? The loveliest thing you can cook for someone who's close to you is about as nice a valentine as you can give.

—Julia Child, chef and television host

The cure for all the ills and wrongs, the cares, the sorrows, and crimes of humanity, all lie in that one word LOVE. It is the divine vitality that produces and restores life. To each and every one of us it gives the power of working miracles, if we will.

—Lydia Maria Child, *Letters from New York*

Love makes no sense at all. But it's the most powerful and amazing force in the entire universe.

—Glenn Close, actress

If you've never been hated by your child, you've never been a parent.

—Bette Davis, actress

Parting is all we know of heaven,
And all we need of hell.

—Emily Dickinson, "My life closed twice before its close"

In the early days of the New England colonies, no more embarrassing or hampering condition, no greater temporal ill, could befall any adult Puritan than to be unmarried.

—Alice Morse Earle, historian

Nothing can bring you peace but yourself.

—Ralph Waldo Emerson, *Self-Reliance*

The way to a man's heart is through his stomach.

—Fanny Fern (Sara Willis), "Willis Parton"

Women revolt at the idea of marrying for the sake of a home, for the sake of a support—of marrying the purse instead of the man. There is no woman here, who, if the question were put to her, would not say, Love is sufficient. She says it is sufficient, and she believes it; yet behind this lies something else, in more than one case in ten.

—Abby Kelley Foster, reformer, "Address to National Woman's Rights Convention"

Love is the irresistible desire to be irresistibly desired.
                                        —Robert Frost, poet

Better to be wounded, a captive and a slave, than always to
walk in armor.
                        —Margaret Fuller, *Summer on the Lakes*

There are only three things worthwhile—fighting, drinking,
and making love.
                        —Katherine Gerould, "The Tortoise"

Love gives naught but itself and takes naught but from
itself. Love possesses not nor would it be possessed; For
love is sufficient unto love.
                                —Kahlil Gibran, *The Prophet*

What good is a friend if you can't make an enemy of him?
                                —William Gillette, actor

Love, whether newly born, or aroused from a
deathlike slumber, must always create sunshine,
filling the heart so full of radiance, this it
overflows upon the outward world.
—Nathaniel Hawthorne, author

I have loved and been in love. There's a big difference.
                                —Katharine Hepburn, actress

If you want to sacrifice the admiration of many men for the criticism of one, go ahead and get married.
—Katharine Houghton Hepburn, activist, to her daughter

Unrequited love is so boring. Weeping under a blue-black sky is for suckers or maniacs.
—Alice Hoffman, *Practical Magic*

The rule of joy and the law of duty seem to me all one.
—Oliver Wendell Holmes Jr., former associate justice of the US Supreme Court, "Speech at Bar Association Dinner, Boston, 1900"

How we love to love things for other people; how we love to have other people love things through our eyes.
—John Irving, *The Cider House Rules*

The flame of love . . . is the most purifying and illuminating thing in this world.
—Harmony Twichell Ives, on her marriage to composer Charles Ives

Maybe the point is that any marriage is work, but you may as well pick work that you like.
—Mindy Kaling, actress

The soul's bliss and suffering are bound together.
—Jane Kenyon, "Twilight: After Haying"

It all ends in tears anyway.

—Jack Kerouac, *The Dharma Bums*

Hug and kiss whoever helped get you—financially, mentally, morally, emotionally—to this day. Parents, mentors, friends, teachers. If you're too uptight to do that, at least do the old handshake thing, but I recommend a hug and a kiss. Don't let the sun go down without saying thank you to someone, and without admitting to yourself that absolutely no one gets this far alone.

—Stephen King, University of
Maine Commencement Address, 2005

Love is like breathing. You take it in and let it out.

—Wally Lamb, *She's Come Undone*

There are times when love seems to be over . . . but these desert times are simply the way to the next oasis which is far more lush and beautiful after the desert crossing.

—Madeleine L'Engle, *Two Part Invention*

If suffering alone taught, all the world would be wise, since everyone suffers.

—Anne Morrow Lindbergh, *Hour of Gold, Hour of Lead*

Things always seem fairer when we look back at them, and it is out of that inaccessible tower of the past that Longing leans and beckons.

—James Russell Lowell, *Literary Essays*

There are things about the single
lifestyle that are very appealing.
—Seth MacFarlane, comedian

Strong affections bring strong afflictions.
—Increase Mather, minister

In life, there are no perfect affections.
—James Merrill, poet

Keep those who truly love you close at all times.
—Jo Dee Messina, singer

Love is not all; it is not meat nor drink
Nor slumber nor a roof against the rain;
Nor yet a floating spar to men that sink.
—Edna St. Vincent Millay, "Love Is Not All"

Maybe love is like luck. You have to go all the way to find it.
—Robert Mitchum, actor

The legal theory is, that marriage makes the husband and
wife one person, and that person is the husband.
—Lucretia Mott, "Discourse on Woman"

People stay married because they want to, not because the doors are locked.

—Paul Newman, actor and philanthropist

Keep some room in your heart for the unimaginable.

—Mary Oliver, "Evidence"

Man is born broken. He lives by mending.
The grace of God is glue.
—Eugene O'Neill, *The Great God Brown*

It is one of the secrets of happiness that you know which battles you can win and which you can't.

—Robert B. Parker, *Potshot*

You don't love someone because they're perfect. You love them in spite of the fact that they're not.

—Jodi Picoult, *My Sister's Keeper*

There is so much hurt in this game of searching for a mate, of testing, trying. And you realize suddenly that you forgot it was a game, and turn away in tears.

—Sylvia Plath, poet

Years of love have been forgot
In the hatred of a minute.

—Edgar Allan Poe, *To M——*

I have realized that mystery is what keeps people away, and I've grown tired of smoke and mirrors. I yearn for the clean, well-lighted place. So let's peek behind the curtain and hail the others like us. The open-faced sandwiches who take risks and live big and smile with all of their teeth. These are the people I want to be around. This is the honest way I want to live and love and write.

—Amy Poehler, *Yes Please*

Love doesn't give you control—it takes control of you.

—Luanne Rice, *Dance with Me*

Love must have wings to fly away from love,
and to fly back again.

—Edwin Arlington Robinson, poet

Never forget that the most powerful force on earth is love.

—Nelson Rockefeller, 41st vice
president of the United States

Marriage partners are to serve each other. Elevate, help, teach, strengthen each other, but above all, *serve*.

—J. D. Salinger, *Raise High the Roof Beam, Carpenters*

Love is never having to say you're sorry.

—Erich Segal, *Love Story*

All who love have lied.

—Anne Sexton, "The Operation"

Love is the one emotion actors allow themselves to believe.

—James Spader, actor

I would say that the surest measure of a man's or a woman's maturity is the harmony, style, joy, and dignity he creates in his marriage, and the pleasure and inspiration he provides for his spouse.

—Benjamin Spock, quoted in *Older & Wiser*

Sentimentality is a failure of feeling.

—Wallace Stevens, *Opus Posthumous*

We believe that personal independence and equal human rights can never be forfeited, except for crime; that marriage should be an equal and permanent partnership, and so recognized by law; that until it is so recognized, married partners should provide against the radical injustice of present laws, by every means in their power.

—Lucy Stone, activist, statement read at her marriage with Henry B. Blackwell, 1855

She works hard for the money
So you better treat her right.

—Donna Summer, "She Works Hard for the Money"

If only we can preserve the real thing—the love of man and woman, the peace of an evening by the fire, the sweetness of music, and the gay sound of children's voices—we shall not have to hear the sound of the world disintegrating into chaos.

—Gladys Taber, *The Book of Stillmeadow*

Aim above morality. Be not simply good; be good for something.

—Henry David Thoreau, *Walden*

Familiarity breeds contempt—and children.

—Mark Twain, *Notebooks*

The first breath of adultery is the freest; after it, constraints aping marriage appear.

—John Updike, *Couples*

It's weird: I've been to prison, I've seen the worst sort of violence and negative s@#t in the streets, but when it comes to putting my heart on the line and letting somebody get to know me in a relationship, it's very difficult.

—Mark Wahlberg, actor

The real marriage of true minds is for any two people to possess a sense of humor or irony pitched in exactly the same key, so that their joint glances on any subject cross like interarching searchlights.

—Edith Wharton, *A Backward Glance*

What is the opposite of two?
A lonely me, a lonely you.
>   —Richard Wilbur, poet, "Opposites"

Laugh, and the world laughs with you;
Weep, and you weep alone.
>   —Ella Wheeler Wilcox, "Solitude"

The fights are the best part of married life.
The rest is merely so-so.
—Thornton Wilder, *The Merchant of Yonkers*

Love is the bond of perfection.
>   —John Winthrop, governor of the Massachusetts
>   Bay Colony, "A Model of Christian Charity"

One's art goes as far and as deep as one's love goes.
>   —Andrew Wyeth, artist

Time may heal wounds, but it does not erase the scars.
>   —Jane Yolen, *Briar Rose*

CHAPTER 11

Separate States and Small Towns

Quotes on the distinctive regions,
big and small, that comprise New England

The already small area of New England is made up of
smaller places—a collection of cities, counties, towns,
neighborhoods, and fenced-in properties. Charming
village houses gather around town greens, and industrial housing gathers around a factory mill. A church,
a skyscraper, a shelf of row-homes. In the 21st century
our six small states have relatively dense populations and
remain fairly united in character and principles. But de-

spite the wishes of people like Henry David Thoreau, we continue to add borders to our worlds and divide ourselves into very real groups.

This can lead to fissures between us, or it can lead to greater connections. As David K. Leff wrote in *The Last Undiscovered Place*, "You feel part of a community if you are part of a community. That is, you may reside anywhere and be counted in the census, but until you participate in some measure you do not truly live in that place." Does a place exist before we care for it? Do you love your house, your neighborhood, your town? What about your watershed, your county, your state? If you love any of these places, then you love New England.

* * *

There arose in Sandwich and in every New England village community the same strife between old residents and new comers as that between the patricians and plebeians of ancient Rome; the old settlers claimed a monopoly of the public land and the new comers demanded a share.

—Herbert Baxter Adams, educator and historian, *The Germanic Origin of New England Towns*

My father and my mother have departed. The charm which has always made this house to me an abode of enchantment is dissolved; and yet my attachment to it, and to the whole region round is stronger than I ever felt before.

—John Quincy Adams, *Diaries*, July 13, 1826

When I grew up, there really was the sense of "Why would you want to live anywhere else?" There's a proudly parochial aspect to Boston.

—Ben Affleck, actor

Poor dull Concord. Nothing colorful has come through here since the Redcoats.

—Louisa May Alcott, *Little Women*

I have lived in New Hampshire nearly forty years, and I am still discovering places and moments of beauty that surprise me. Sometimes it may be seeing the same setting—a country road, a hillside, a meadow—in different light or in a different season.

—Mel Allen, editor of *Yankee*

The factory is a good prevention against quaintness; it removes from the village a possibly "cute" edge.

—Anthony Bailey, *In the Village*

I'm from western Massachusetts, where like, the cows are.

—Elizabeth Banks, actress

East and ahead of the coast of North America, some thirty miles and more from the inner shores of Massachusetts, there stands in the open Atlantic the last fragment of an ancient and vanished land.

—Henry Beston, *The Outermost House*

A New Hampshire swamp is full of attractions at all seasons.
—Frank Bolles, *At the North of Bearcamp Water*

The rocky land between Cape Elizabeth and East Quoddy
Head was once a country apart from other countries.
—Gerald Warner Brace, *Between Wind and Water*

All in all, Vermont is a jewel state, small but precious.
—Pearl S. Buck, from *Pearl Buck's America*

The place of exciting innovation—where the action is—
that's Rhode Island.
—Donald Carcieri, 73rd governor of Rhode Island

Well I love that dirty water
Oh, Boston, you're my home.
—E. Cobb, performed by the Standells, "Dirty Water"

If the spirit of liberty should vanish in other parts of the
union, and support of our institutions should languish, it
could all be replenished from the generous store held by the
people of this brave little state of Vermont.
—Calvin Coolidge, 30th president of the United States,
Address in Bennington, Vermont, September 9, 1928

There's such an odd, eclectic group of people that make up the town of Plymouth, New Hampshire. I don't think I could avoid not coming out of there with a pretty good sense of humor.

—Eliza Coupe, actress

The country towns here in New England all bear a family resemblance to one another, but they also have individual characters that can be learned only by living in them.

—Malcolm Cowley, "Town Report, 1942,"
in *New Republic*

It takes trigonometry, solid geography, and calculus to get at Vermont.

—Charles Edward Crane, *Let Me Show You Vermont*

It was a very charming, comfortable old town— this Boston of uncrowded shops and untroubled self-respect which, in 1822, reluctantly allowed itself to be made into a city.

—Mary Caroline Crawford,
Romantic Days in Old Boston

Provincetown is, has always been, an eccentrics' sanctuary, more or less the way other places are bird sanctuaries or wild game preserves. It is the only small town I know of where those who live unconventionally seem to outnumber those who live within the prescribed boundaries of home and licensed marriage, respectable jobs and biological children. It is where people who were the outcasts and untouchables in other towns can become prominent members of society.

—Michael Cunningham, *Land's End*

In Burlington, I can call anyone and learn from their experience. The degrees of separation are lessened here. There's a shared Vermontiness.

—Marguerite Dibble, founder of Game Theory

It storms in Amherst five days—it snows, and then it rains, and then soft fogs like veils hang on all the houses, and then the days turn Topaz, like a lady's pin.

—Emily Dickinson, "Letter to Mrs. Samuel Bowles, December 10, 1859"

I live in a capital of light.

—Mark Doty, on Provincetown, Massachusetts, *Still Life with Oysters and Lemon*

Mr. Johnson assured me that no slaveholder could take a slave from New Bedford; that there were men there who would lay down their lives, before such an outrage could be perpetuated.

—Frederick Douglass, *My Bondage and My Freedom*

Monhegan [Island] is known to be the resort or asylum of pirates, smugglers, or mutineers, centuries ago. If what we do not know about it could be unearthed, what an interesting chapter it would make.

—Samuel Adams Drake, *The Pine-Tree Coast*

I have visited several countries, and I like my own the best. I have been in all the States of the Union, and Connecticut is the best State; Windsor is the pleasantest town in the State of Connecticut and I have the pleasantest place in Windsor. I am content, perfectly content, to die on the banks of the Connecticut.

—Oliver Ellsworth, 3rd chief justice of the US Supreme Court

To me, Boston is friends, family, and home . . . I've thought a lot about what home means. For me, it's where the brain stops asking so many questions.

—Chris Evans, actor

When people who have never lived in New Hampshire or Vermont visit here, they often say they feel like they've come home. Our urban center, commercial districts, small villages and industrial enterprises are set amid farmlands and forests. This is a landscape in which the natural and built environments are balanced on a human scale.

—Richard J. Eward, *Proud to Live Here*

No Vermont town ever let anybody in it starve.

—Dorothy Canfield Fisher, author

The Vermont mountains stretch extended straight; New Hampshire mountains curl up in a coil.

—Robert Frost, poet

Small towns make up for their lack of people by having everyone be more interesting.

—Doris "Granny D" Haddock, activist

New England is quite as large a lump of earth as my heart can really take in.

—Nathaniel Hawthorne, author

In New England we have but to step across the border of the adjoining state to feel at once the sharp differentiation, the geological cut-off which expresses itself in the general aspect of the land and in the thousand and one simple facts of its topography, its flora, its fauna, its people, its customs, its coast, its climate, and its industries.

—Helen Henderson, *A Loiterer in New England*

At our arrival at New Plymouth, in New England, we found all our friends and planters in good health, though they were left sick and weak, with very small means; the Indians round about us peaceable and friendly; the country very pleasant and temperate, yielding naturally, of itself, great store of fruits, as vines of diverse sorts, in great abundance. There is likewise walnuts, chestnuts, small nuts and plums, with much variety of flowers, roots and herbs, no less pleasant than wholesome and profitable. No place hath more gooseberries and strawberries, nor better.

—William Hilton, "Letter to His Family, 1621"

Maine is not a death cult. I mean, it is, but it's a slow one. It creeps in like the tide, and without your even noticing, the ground around you is swallowed by water until it's gone.

—John Hodgman, comedian, *Vacationland: True Stories from Painful Beaches*

That's all I claim for Boston—that it is the thinking center of the continent, and therefore of the planet.

—Oliver Wendell Holmes Sr., *The Professor at the Breakfast-Table*

Boston is an oasis in the desert, a place where the larger proportion of people are loving, rational and happy.
—Julia Ward Howe, author

The atmospheric tone, the careful selection of ingredients, your pleasant sense of a certain climatic ripeness—these are the real charm of Newport, and the secret of her supremacy.
—Henry James, "Newport"

In my own native state of Massachusetts, the battle for American freedom was begun by the thousands of farmers and tradesmen who made up the Minute Men—citizens who were ready to defend their liberty at a moment's notice. Today we need a nation of minute men; citizens who are not only prepared to take up arms, but citizens who regard the preservation of freedom as a basic purpose of their daily life and who are willing to consciously work and sacrifice for that freedom. The cause of liberty, the cause of America, cannot succeed with any lesser effort.
—John F. Kennedy, 35th president of the United States, "Commemorative Message on Roosevelt Day"

It is New Hampshire out here,
It is nearly the dawn.
The song of the whippoorwill stops
And the dimension of depth seizes everything.
—Galway Kinnell, "Flower Herding on Mount Monadnock"

You could cut the brackish winds with a knife here in Nantucket.

—Robert Lowell, "The Quaker Graveyard at Nantucket"

Our state's beautiful natural environment is part of why we all love and live in New Hampshire. It is also one of our state's most important economic assets.

—John Lynch, 80th governor of New Hampshire

Sometimes here on Pequod Island and back again on Beacon Street, I have the most curious delusion that our world may be a little narrow. I cannot avoid the impression that something has gone out of it (what, I do not know), and that our little world moves in an orbit of its own, again one of those confounded circles, or possibly an ellipse. Do you suppose that it moves without any relation to anything else? That it is broken off from some greater planet like the moon? We talk of life, we talk of art, but do we actually know anything about either? Have any of us really lived?

—John P. Marquand, *The Late George Apley*

A whale ship was my Yale and my Harvard.

—Herman Melville, *Moby-Dick*

The place is infused with time; everywhere you look, east or west, north or south, there is history; there are stories, and ghosts, and bear spirits.

—John Hanson Mitchell, *Ceremonial Time, Fifteen Thousand Years on One Square Mile*

[It would not be long] ere the whole surface of this
country would be channeled for those nerves which are
to diffuse, with the speed of thought, a knowledge of all
that is occurring throughout the land, making, in fact, one
neighborhood of the whole country.

—Samuel F. B. Morse, inventor,
Samuel F. B. Morse: His Letters and Journals

The ballpark is the star. In the age of Tris Speaker and Babe
Ruth, the era of Jimmie Foxx and Ted Williams, through
the empty-seats epoch of Don Buddin and Willie Tasby
and unto the decades of Carl Yastrzemski and Jim Rice, the
ballpark is the star. A crazy-quilt violation of city planning
principles, an irregular pile of architecture, a menace to
marketing consultants, Fenway Park works. It works as a
symbol of New England's pride, as a repository of evergreen
hopes, as a tabernacle of lost innocence. It works as a place
to watch baseball.

—Martin Nolan, journalist, *Boston Globe*

Connecticut was a place where you could put on a new life,
as though it were a skin you'd just picked out.

—Cathie Pelletier, *The Weight of Winter*

Why do I live in Connecticut? As an artist and a writer I need
New York for the American Museum of Natural History and
Boston for Houghton Mifflin, my publisher. But as a naturalist
I prefer to live as far from either city as I can manage.

—Roger Tory Peterson, *All Things Reconsidered*

You can stand there on the rocks between the sea and
the forest of spruce and fir and feel, backing you up, the
whole expanse and power of this country, reaching away
behind you to the Pacific and the Gulf of Mexico. It's quite a
sensation.
              —Louise Dickinson Rich, *The Coast of Maine*

The city replaced the natural wilderness
in American belief as the prime *locus* of
opportunity, adventure, and success, just as
industry replaced agriculture as the primary
means to success.
              —James Oliver Robertson,
              American Myth, American Reality

I found community here.
    —Vince Rooney, co-owner of Falls General Store, on why
                        he moved from Long Island to Vermont

The obvious advantage of living in a little country is that one
may get to know it all.
              —Odell Shepard, *The Harvest of a Quiet Eye*

My heart is on the mountain still
Where'er my steps may be;
Vermont, O maiden of the hills,
My heart is still with thee.
              —Wendell Phillips Stafford, judge

There is nothing that gives the feel of
Connecticut like coming home to it.
—Wallace Stevens, *Opus Posthumous*

The small town endures as the national attic of American
social and spatial consciousness, a sort of frame through
which further vistas are invariably viewed and twisted to fit.
—John Stilgoe, *Outside Lies Magic*

I remember standing often in the door of our house and
looking over a distant horizon, where Mount Tom reared
its round blue head against the sky, and the Great and Little
Ponds, as they were called, gleamed out amid a steel-blue
sea of distant pine groves. To the west of us rose a smooth-
bosomed hill called Prospect Hill; and many a pensive,
wondering hour have I sat at our play-room window,
watching the glory of the wonderful sunsets that used to
burn themselves out, amid voluminous wreathings, or
castellated turrets of clouds—vaporous pageantry proper to
a mountainous region.
—Harriet Beecher Stowe,
"Earliest Remembrances of Litchfield"

Cape Cod is the bared and bended arm of Massachusetts:
the shoulder is at Buzzard's Bay; the elbow, or crazy-bone,
at Cape Mallebarre; the wrist at Truro; and the sandy fist
at Provincetown,—behind which the State stands on her
guard, with her back to the Green Mountains, and her feet
planted on the floor of the ocean, like an athlete protecting

172

her Bay,—boxing with northwest storms, and, ever and anon, heaving up her Atlantic adversary from the lap of earth,—ready to thrust forward her other fist, which keeps guard the while upon her breast at Cape Ann.

—Henry David Thoreau, *Cape Cod*

I'm lucky to have been raised in the most beautiful place, Amherst, Massachusetts, state of my heart. I'm more patriotic to Massachusetts than to almost any other place.

—Uma Thurman, actress

In Boston they ask, how much does he know? In New York, how much is he worth? In Philadelphia, who were his parents?

—Mark Twain, author

I grew up in New Hampshire. My closest neighbor was a mile away. The deer and the raccoons were my friends. So, I would spend time walking through the woods, looking for the most beautiful tropical thing that can survive the winter in the woods in New Hampshire.

—Steven Tyler, singer

Fenway Park, in Boston, is a lyric little bandbox of a ballpark. Everything is painted green and seems in curiously sharp focus, like the inside of an old-fashioned peeping-type Easter egg . . . a compromise between Man's Euclidean determinations and Nature's beguiling irregularities.

—John Updike, "Hub Fans Bid Kid Adieu"

Our houses are our biographies, the stories of our defeats and victories.

—Mary Heaton Vorse, journalist
and activist, *Time and the Town*

Even as I talk I can see it and smell it and feel it. It's a special, insular, quiet, healing, glorious place. And year after year after year, you not only see your kids and grandchildren grow, but you see everybody else's kids, the same people, grow. There's a strange continuity to life on the Vineyard.

—Mike Wallace, broadcast journalist

To own a bit of ground, to scratch it with a hoe, to plant seeds, and watch the renewal of life—this is the commonest delight of the race, the most satisfactory thing man can do.

—Charles Dudley Warner, *My Summer in a Garden*

Once in everyone's life there is apt to be a period when he is fully awake, instead of half asleep. I think of those five years in Maine as the time when this happened to me . . . I was suddenly seeing, feeling, and listening as a child sees, feels, and listens. It was one of those rare interludes that can never be repeated, a time of enchantment.

—E. B. White, *One Man's Meat*

I found—or thought I found—that Newport, Rhode Island, presented nine cities, some superimposed, some having very little relation with the others—variously beautiful, impressive, absurd, commonplace, and one very nearly squalid.
—Thornton Wilder, *Theophilus North*

It's a small world, but I wouldn't want to paint it.
—Steven Wright, comedian

There's a quality of life in Maine which is this singular and unique. I think. It's absolutely a world onto itself.
—Jamie Wyeth, artist

Massachusetts has been the wheel within New England, and Boston the wheel within Massachusetts. Boston therefore is often called the "hub of the world," since it has been the source and fountain of the ideas that have reared and made America.
—Reverend F. B. Zinckle,
Last Winter in the United States

CHAPTER 12

Life and Death

Quotes about our mortality
and how best to use it

Death often seems close by in New England. The browned autumn leaves that pile against stone walls, the bare branches weighted with heavy snow, ready to crack. The ruins of our mills, the husks of our elms, the slow decay of our history. And so many cemeteries, more than any other area of the country, full of drowned fishermen, poisoned factory workers, consumptive poets. They gather around us, whispering something dark and dreary. "If there's a light at the end of the tunnel," said Robert Lowell, "it's the light of the oncoming train."

And yet there remains something immortal and unshakable here, too, a rooted belief, hard and true as old granite. That our little lives whirling in the endless void of space mean something after all. That work or love or faith will sustain us. That what we do matters. And if not? Well, we're New Englanders, so we do it anyway, we cook our dinner, phone a friend, give ourselves to the whirlwind. We live our lives. As Stephen King wrote in *Rita Hayworth and Shawshank Redemption*, "Get busy living or get busy dying." That's goddamn right.

* * *

Only on the edge of the grave can man conclude anything.
—Henry Adams, *The Education of Henry Adams*

Old minds are like old horses; you must exercise them if you wish to keep them in working order.
—John Adams, 2nd president of the United States

Time is one's best friend, teaching
best of all the wisdom of silence.
—Amos Bronson Alcott, *Table Talk*

This is the day. You might have died
And never seen Rowayton in the rain,
Or morning glories bloom in Darien.
This is the day you might have died.
—Dick Allen, "On the New Haven Line"

Backward, turn backward, O Time, in your flight,
Make me a child again, just for tonight!
—Elizabeth Akers Allen, "Rock Me to Sleep"

Man is an infant still, and slow and late
Must form and fix his adolescent state,
Mature his manhood, and at last behold
His reason ripen and his force unfold.
                    —Joel Barlow, diplomat, *The Columbiad*

Dear brethren, our ship is sailing fast. We shall soon hear
the rasping of the shallows, and the commotion overhead
which bespeaks the port in view. When it comes to that,
how will you feel? Are you a stranger, or a convict, or are
you going home? Brethren, we are all sailing home; and by
and by, when we are not thinking of it, some shadowy thing
(men call it death), at midnight, will pass by, and will call us
by name, and will say, "I have a message for you from home;
God wants you; heaven waits for you."
                    —Henry Ward Beecher, minister

The art of losing isn't hard to master.
                    —Elizabeth Bishop, "One Art"

We know not where the infant's forces come from, nor
where the dying man's energy goes to, but if Nature
teaches us anything, it teaches us that forces such as these
are eternal in the same sense that matter is eternal and
space endless.
                    —Frank Bolles, *At the North of Bearcamp Water*

Memories, after all, are the roots of understanding. Without a yesterday, today is meaningless.

—Hal Borland, *Countryman: A Summary of Belief*

So live, that when thy summons comes to join
The innumerable caravan, which moves
To that mysterious realm, where each shall take
His chamber in the silent halls of death,
Thou go not, like the quarry-slave at night,
Scourged to his dungeon, but, sustained and soothed
By an unfaltering trust, approach thy grave,
Like one who wraps the drapery of his couch
About him, and lies down to pleasant dreams.

—William Cullen Bryant, "Thanatopsis"

The young do not know enough to be prudent, and so they attempt the impossible, and achieve it, generation after generation.

—Pearl S. Buck, author

I think we too often make choices based on the safety of cynicism, and what we're led to is a life not fully lived. Cynicism is fear, and it's worse than fear—it's active disengagement.

—Ken Burns, filmmaker

It is not death therefore that is burdensome, but the fear of death.

—Ambrose Burnside, Civil War general and
30th governor of Rhode Island

Life has all sorts of hills and valleys, and sometimes you don't end up doing what you had your heart set out on, but sometimes that's even better.

—Ruth Buzzi, actress and comedian

Have little care that Life is brief,
And less that Art is long.
Success is in the silences
Though Fame is in the song.

—Bliss Carman, "Envoy"

Life is available to anyone no matter what age. All you have to do is grab it.

—Art Carney, comedian

There is no knowing what a stretch of pain and misery the human mind is capable of contemplating when it is wrought upon by the anxieties of preservation; nor what pangs and weaknesses the body is able to endure, until they are visited upon it; and when at last deliverance comes, when the dream of hope is realized, unspeakable gratitude takes possession of the soul, and tears of joy choke the utterance.

—Owen Chase, sailor, *Narrative of the Most
Extraordinary and Distressing Shipwreck
of the Whale-Ship Essex, of Nantucket*

Life itself is the proper binge.
　　　　　　—Julia Child, chef and television host

You've got to go through it to get to the end of it.
　　　　—Suzanne Collins, *The Hunger Games: Catching Fire*

Those who trust to chance must abide
by the results of chance.
—Calvin Coolidge, 30th president
of the United States

It doesn't matter how old you are, I think, just as long as
you feel good and feel great about what you're doing.
　　　　　　　　—Jill Craybas, tennis player

Unbeing dead isn't being alive.
　　　　　　　　—e. e. cummings, *73 Poems*

I see not in reason how we shall escape even the gaspings of
hunger-starved persons; but God can do much, and His will
be done. It is better for me to die than now for me to bear
it, which I do daily and expect it hourly, having received the
sentence of death both within me and without me.
—Robert Cushman, "Letter to Edward Southworth, 1620"

Death is at all times solemn, but never so much so as at sea.
　　　　　　　—Richard Henry Dana Jr., lawyer,
　　　　　　　　　　Two Years Before the Mast

That it will never come again
Is what makes life so sweet.
—Emily Dickinson, "Poem no. 1741"

How we spend our days is, of course, how we spend our lives.
—Annie Dillard, *The Writing Life*

I have learned to live each day as it comes, and not to
borrow trouble by dreading tomorrow.
—Dorothea Dix, mental health activist

One thing alone I charge you. As you live, believe in life!
—W. E. B. Du Bois, last words

Spirit is the real and eternal; matter is the unreal and temporal.
—Mary Baker Eddy, religious leader,
Science and Health with Key to the Scriptures

Resolved, never to do anything which I should be afraid to
do if it were the last hour of my life.
—Jonathan Edwards, preacher and theologian,
Seventy Resolutions

The fact that human conscience remains partially infantile
throughout our life is the core of human tragedy.
—Erik Erikson, psychologist, *Childhood and Society*

Lots of old people don't get wise, but you don't get wise
unless you age.

—Joan Erikson, dance ethnographer

But for life the universe were nothing; and all that has life
requires nourishment.

—Fannie Farmer, chef, *The Boston
Cooking-School Cook Book*

Each unmeasured moment is the extension
of a lease I never held, a gift whose very
breadth and extent removes any
possible anxiety over losing it.

—Robert Finch, author and
radio commentator, *The Primal Place*

When a man or a woman holds fast to youth, even if
successfully, there is something of the pitiful and the tragic
involved. It is the everlasting struggle of the soul to retain
the joy of earth, whose fleeing distinguishes it from heaven,
and whose retention is not accomplished without an inner
knowledge of its futility.

—Mary E. Wilkins Freeman, "The Amethyst Comb"

In three words I can sum up everything I've learned about
life—It goes on.

—Robert Frost, poet

The illusion that times that were are better than those that are, has probably pervaded all ages.

—Horace Greeley, journalist, *The American Conflict*

Here, in Maine, every stone is a skull and you live close to your own death. Where, you ask yourself, where indeed will I be buried? That is the power of those old villages: to remind you of stasis.

—Elizabeth Hardwick, *The Collected
Essays of Elizabeth Hardwick*

Meet life's terms but never accept them.

—Michael S. Harper, poet

We sometimes congratulate ourselves at the moment of waking from a troubled dream; it may be so the moment after death.

—Nathaniel Hawthorne, *Journal*, October 25, 1836

Everything lies ready to be, for an instant, a thousand years, and though we may be able to count and measure everything we meet, the great, cosmic swing of the tides takes us beyond all measurement.

—John Hay, *The Undiscovered Country*

Without discipline, there's no life at all.

—Katharine Hepburn, actress

I wonder what we will do this year, what it will do with us, and what we and life will create during the twelve months ahead . . . A new year is a gift, a small piece of infinity, to do with as we will.

—Jean Hersey, *The Shape of a Year*

This life's hard, but it's harder if you're stupid.
—George V. Higgins,
The Friends of Eddie Coyle

Insanity is often the logic of an accurate mind overtasked.
—Oliver Wendell Holmes Sr.,
The Autocrat of the Breakfast Table

The sun will not rise or set without my notice, and thanks.
—Winslow Homer, painter

Life passes, but the conditions of life do not.
—Julia Ward Howe, *Beyond the Veil*

You only grow by coming to the end of something and by beginning something else.
—John Irving, *The World According to Garp*

Life itself leaves you with a question—it asks you questions.
—Henry James, author

Be not afraid of life. Believe that life is worth living, and
your belief will help create the fact.
　　　　　—William James, philosopher and psychologist,
The Will to Believe

Life is either a daring adventure, or nothing.
　　　—Helen Keller, disability rights activist, *The Open Door*

Don't take life so serious, son . . .
it ain't no how permanent.
—Walt Kelly, cartoonist, *Pogo*

Let it come, as it will, and don't
be afraid. God does not leave us
comfortless, so let evening come.
　　　　　　　—Jane Kenyon, "Let Evening Come"

The road is life.
　　　　　　　—Jack Kerouac, *On the Road*

So late we get smart, so soon we get old.
　　　　　　　—Fred King, Maine guide

Into each life some rain must fall,
Some days must be dark and dreary.
　　　—Henry Wadsworth Longfellow, "The Rainy Day"

That is not dead which can eternal lie,
And with strange aeons even death may die.
                          —H. P. Lovecraft, "The Nameless City"

Youth condemns; maturity condones.
                          —Amy Lowell, *Tendencies in
                          Modern American Poetry*

But life is sweet, though all that makes it sweet
Lessen like sound of friends' departing feet;
And Death is beautiful as feet of friend
Coming with welcome at our journey's end.
  —James Russell Lowell, *An Epistle to George William Curtis*

This is death
To die and know it.
                          —Robert Lowell, "Mr. Edwards and the Spider"

You will never have more energy or enthusiasm, hair, or
brain cells than you have today.
                          —Ray Magliozzi, radio host, *Car Talk*

Generosity during life is a very different thing from
generosity in the hour of death; one proceeds from genuine
liberality and benevolence, the other from pride or fear.
                          —Horace Mann, educator

None but a good man is really a living man, and the more good any man does, the more he really lives. All the rest is death, or belongs to it.

—Cotton Mather, minister, *Bonifacius*

Life's a voyage that's homeward bound.

—Herman Melville, author

Always that same old story—
Father Time and Mother Earth,
A marriage on the rocks.

—James Merrill, "The Broken Home"

My candle burns at both ends;
It will not last the night;
But, oh, my foes, and oh, my friends—
It gives a lovely light.

—Edna St. Vincent Millay, "First Fig"

How few the days are that hold the mind in place; like tapestry hanging on four or five hooks. Especially the day you stop becoming; the day you merely are.

—Arthur Miller, playwright

A life is like a garden. Perfect moments can be had, but not preserved, except in memory.
—Leonard Nimoy, actor

There are few things more liberating in life than having your worst fear realized.

> —Conan O'Brien, Commencement Address
> at Dartmouth College, 2011

Instructions for living a life.
Pay attention.
Be astonished.
Tell about it.

> —Mary Oliver, "Sometimes"

Life is for each man a solitary cell whose walls are mirrors.

> —Eugene O'Neill, *Lazarus Laughed*

I am ambitious, but it's a long-range thing with me. I have my confidential sights on a star, but there's half a lifetime to get to it. Meanwhile I keep my eyes open and am well dressed.

> —Grace Paley, "The Contest"

What if it turns out that a life isn't defined by who you belong to, or where you came from, by what you wished for or whom you've lost, but instead by the moments you spend getting from each of these places to the next?

> —Jodi Picoult, *Vanishing Acts*

Dying, is an art, like everything else.

> —Sylvia Plath, "Lady Lazarus"

And as, in ethics, Evil is a consequence of Good, so, in fact, out of Joy is sorrow born. Either the memory of past bliss is the anguish of to-day, or the agonies which *are*, have their origin in the ecstasies which *might have been*.

—Edgar Allan Poe, "Berenice"

Hopefully as you get older, you start to learn how to live with your demon.

—Amy Poehler, *Yes Please*

Nature is strictly moral. There is no attempt to cheat the Earth my means of steel vault of bronze coffin. I hope that when I die I too may be permitted to pay at once my oldest outstanding debt, to restore promptly the minerals and salts that have been lent to me for the little while that I have use for blood and bone and flesh.

—Louise Dickinson Rich, author

Life is the game that must be played.

—Edwin Arlington Robinson, "Ballad by the Fire"

Life is a gift horse, in my opinion.

—J. D. Salinger, "Teddy"

Joy multiplies when it is shared among friends, but grief diminishes with every division. That is life.

—R. A. Salvatore, *Exile*

There is no cure for birth and
death save to enjoy the interval.
—George Santayana, *Soliloquies in England*

Wrinkles on a beloved's face, the body after death, are
mortal lessons. He who shrinks from their contemplation
is like a dandy sniffing a vinegar-soaked hanky lest he catch
the rank whiff of the poor.
—Richard Selzer, surgeon, author

There must be more to life than having everything.
—Maurice Sendak, illustrator

Beauty is a simple passion,
But, oh my friends, in the end
You will dance the fire dance in iron shoes.
—Anne Sexton, "Snow White and the Seven Dwarfs"

It is a better thing to travel hopefully than to arrive, for
beyond every bend there is a lurking mystery and a romantic
distance to lure us on and on.
—Odell Shepard, *The Harvest of a Quiet Eye*

Let be be finale of seem
The only emperor is the emperor of ice cream.
—Wallace Stevens, "The Emperor of Ice Cream"

Death is an endless night so awful to contemplate that it can make us love life and value it with such passion that it may be the ultimate cause of all joy and all art.

—Paul Theroux, *Hockney's Alphabet, D Is for Death*

Let us spend one day as deliberately as Nature, and not be thrown off the track by every nutshell and mosquito's wing that falls on the rails.

—Henry David Thoreau, *Walden*

From birth to age eighteen, a girl needs good parents. From eighteen to thirty-five, she needs good looks. From thirty-five to fifty-five, she needs a good personality. From fifty-five on, she needs good cash.

—Sophie Tucker, singer

All you need in this life is ignorance and confidence; then success is sure.

—Mark Twain, "Letter to Mrs. Foote"

To die should be the most interesting journey of all the journeys a person can take.

—Janwillem van de Wetering, author

What small potatoes we all are, compared with what we might be!

—Charles Dudley Warner, *My Summer in a Garden*

In spite of illness, in spite even of the arch-enemy sorrow, one *can* remain alive long past the usual date of disintegration if one is unafraid of change, insatiable in intellectual curiosity, interested in big things, and happy in small ways.

—Edith Wharton, *A Backward Glance*

Imagination! who can sing thy force?
Or who describe the swiftness of thy course?
Soaring through air to find the bright abode,
Th' empyreal place of the thund'ring God,
We on thy pinions can surpass the wind,
And leave the rolling universe behind.

—Phillis Wheatley, "On Imagination"

Life is like writing with a pen. You can cross out your past but you can't erase it.

—E. B. White, author

When we don't enjoy what we do, we only nick the surface of our potential.

—Dennis Wholey, television host, *The Miracle of Change*

Now there are some things we all know, but we don't take'm out and look at'm very often. We all know that something is eternal. And it ain't houses and it ain't names, and it ain't earth, and it ain't even the stars . . . everybody knows in their bones that something is eternal, and that something has to do with human beings.

—Thornton Wilder, *Our Town*

Experience is something you don't
get until just after you need it.
—Steven Wright, comedian

INDEX

M

MacFarlane, Seth, 153
Mack, Connie, 105
MacLeish, Archibald, 42, 56, 91
Magliozzi, Ray, 187
Magliozzi, Tom, 10, 26, 77
Mailer, Norman, 105
Malcolm X, 42, 124
Mann, Horace, 10, 77, 187
Mansfield, Howard, 56
Marciano, Rocky, 105
Marquand, John P., 124, 169
Marsh, George Perkins, 56
Martineau, Harriet, 137
Martinez, Pedro, 138
Mather, Cotton, 10, 26, 124, 188
Mather, Increase, 124, 153
McAuliffe, Christa, 124
McCloskey, Robert, 10
McCullough, David, 10, 106
McKay, Claude, 138
McKibben, Bill, 57
McLaughlin, John, 77
Melville, Herman, 10, 57, 77, 91, 138, 169, 188
Merrill, James, 42, 57, 153, 188
Messervy, Julie Moir, 57
Messina, Jo Dee, 26, 153
Miantunnomoh, 77
Millay, Edna St. Vincent, 98, 153, 188
Miller, Arthur, 42, 106, 138, 188
Miller, Bode, 106
Miller, Rebecca, 78
Mitchell, George J., 78
Mitchell, John Hanson, 169
Mitchum, Robert, 153
Morath, Inge, 106
Morgan, Edmund, 139
Morgan, Lewis H., 139
Morgan, John Pierpont, Sr., 11

Morrissey, Bill, 106
Morse, Samuel F. B., 170
Motley, John Lothrop, 78
Mott, Lucretia, 153
Mucci, Henry, 42
Muir, Diana, 78, 91
Murakami, Haruki, 11, 42, 91
Murray, Judith Sargent, 43, 125
Muskie, Edmund, 26, 78

N

Naismith, James, 106
Neal, John, 26, 43
Nearing, Scott and Helen, 107
Nelson, Marilyn, 58, 92
Newman, Paul, 27, 154
Nichols, Rachel, 58, 107
Nimoy, Leonard, 188
Noble, William Henry, 43
Nolan, Martin, 170
Norris, Gunilla, 92
Norton, Charles Eliot, 125

O

O'Brien, Conan, 11, 189
Occum, Samson, 78
Oliver, Mary, 92, 154, 189
Olmsted, Frederick Law, 58, 107
O'Neill, Eugene, 11, 27, 58, 154, 189
O'Neill, Thomas P. "Tip," Jr., 79
O'Rourke, Jim, 107
O'Rourke, P. J., 27
Ortiz, David, 78, 102, 107
Osborne, Terry, 58
Otis, Jr., James, 43

P

Paley, Grace, 79, 189
Parcak, Sarah, 59
Parcells, Bill, 11

Steele, Thomas Sedgwick, 61
Stevens, Wallace, 44, 61, 156, 172, 191
Stevenson, Parker, 141
Stewart, Martha, 80, 126
Stiles, Ezra, 126
Stilgoe, John, 61, 172
Stone, Lucy, 126, 156
Stookey, Paul, 14
Stowe, Harriet Beecher, 126, 172
Stratton, Charles, 141
Strout, Elizabeth, 29, 142
Stuart, Gilbert, 109
Styron, William, 109
Sullivan, Anne, 14
Summer, Donna, 156
Sumner, Charles, 127

T
Taber, Gladys, 157
Taibbi, Matt, 142
Talbot, Gerald, 127
Tantaquidgeon, Harold, 14
Tartt, Donna, 142
Taylor, James, 62
Teale, Edwin Way, 29, 62
Tewksbury, Bob, 110
Thaxter, Celia, 62
Thayer, Ernest L., 110
Theroux, Paul, 14, 94, 192
Thompson, Brigadier Samuel, 127
Thoreau, Henry David, 14, 29, 44, 62, 80, 94, 110, 127, 157, 160, 173, 192
Thorson, Robert, 63
Thurman, Uma, 173
Thurston, Laura Hawley, 63
Trollope, Frances, 142
Tsai, Ming, 110
Tuchman, Barbara, 45
Tucker, Sophie, 192

Twain, Mark, 1, 15, 29, 45, 83, 94, 110, 143, 157, 173, 192
Tyler, Steven, 15, 173

U
Updike, John, 30, 45, 110, 157, 173

V
Vallee, Rudy, 15
van de Wetering, Janwillem, 192
Verrill, A. Hyatt, 63
Voight, Ellen Bryant, 94
von Bismarck, Otto, 143
Vonnegut, Kurt, 2, 111, 143
von Trapp, Maria Augusta, 111, 143
Vorse, Mary Heaton, 174

W
Wahlberg, Mark, 157
Wallace, Mike, 174
Walters, Barbara, 15
Ward, Artemus, 30, 45, 80
Warner, Charles Dudley, 30, 81, 95, 174, 193
Warren, Elizabeth, 81
Warren, Joseph, 46
Webster, Daniel, 15, 46, 81, 127
Webster, Noah, 35, 46, 81, 111, 128, 143
West, Dorothy, 30
Wharton, Edith, 15, 81, 95, 111, 157, 193
Wheatley, Phillis, 15, 193
Wheeler, Cheryl, 95
Whipple, William, 46
Whistler, James McNeill, 16
White, Brian J., 82
White, E. B., 16, 95, 144, 174, 193
White, Ellen G., 16, 128
Whitman, Sarah Helen, 95
Whitman, Walt, 144

Whittier, John Greenleaf, 16, 31, 47, 96
Wholey, Dennis, 193
Wilbur, Richard, 63, 158
Wilcox, Ella Wheeler, 158
Wilder, Thornton, 146, 158, 175, 194
Williams, Dick, 111
Williams, Roger, 16, 64, 128
Williams, Ted, 16, 111, 170
Wilson, Woodrow, 144
Winslow, Edward, 112
Winthrop, John, 30, 47, 82, 158

Winthrop, Theodore, 47
Woods, James, 17
Wright, Steven, 17, 175, 194
Wyeth, Andrew, 96, 158
Wyeth, Jamie, 31, 64, 175
Wyeth, N .C., 17, 112

Y
Yolen, Jane, 158

Z
Zinckle, Reverend F. B., 175